Scott Foresman
Science

See learning in a whole new light

PEARSON
Scott Foresman

Editorial Offices: Glenview, Illinois • Parsippany, New Jersey •
Sales Offices: Needham, Massachusetts • Duluth, Georgia • Glenview, Illinois •
Coppell, Texas • Sacramento, California • Mesa, Arizona
www.sfsuccessnet.com

Series Authors

Dr. Timothy Cooney
Professor of Earth Science and Science Education
University of Northern Iowa (UNI)
Cedar Falls, Iowa

Dr. Jim Cummins
Professor
Department of Curriculum, Teaching, and Learning
University of Toronto
Toronto, Canada

Dr. James Flood
Distinguished Professor of Literacy and Language
School of Teacher Education
San Diego State University.
San Diego, California

Barbara Kay Foots, M.Ed.
Science Education Consultant
Houston, Texas

Dr. M. Jenice Goldston
Associate Professor of Science Education
Department of Elementary Education Programs
University of Alabama
Tuscaloosa, Alabama

Dr. Shirley Gholston Key
Associate Professor of Science Education
Instruction and Curriculum Leadership Department
College of Education
University of Memphis
Memphis, Tennessee

Dr. Diane Lapp
Distinguished Professor of Reading and Language Arts in Teacher Education
San Diego State University
San Diego, California

Sheryl A. Mercier
Classroom Teacher
Dunlap Elementary School
Dunlap, California

Dr. Karen L. Ostlund
Director
UTeach, College of Natural Sciences
The University of Texas at Austin
Austin, Texas

Dr. Nancy Romance
Professor of Science Education & Principal Investigator
NSF/IERI Science IDEAS Project
Charles E. Schmidt College of Science
Florida Atlantic University
Boca Raton, Florida

Dr. William Tate
Chair and Professor of Education and Applied Statistics
Department of Education
Washington University
St. Louis, Missouri

Dr. Kathryn C. Thornton
Professor
School of Engineering and Applied Science
University of Virginia
Charlottesville, Virginia

Dr. Leon Ukens
Professor of Science Education
Department of Physics, Astronomy, and Geosciences
Towson University
Towson, Maryland

Steve Weinberg
Consultant
Connecticut Center for Advanced Technology
East Hartford, Connecticut

ISBN: 0-328-10002-1 (SVE); ISBN: 0-328-15672-8 (A); ISBN: 0-328-15678-7 (B);
ISBN: 0-328-15684-1 (C); ISBN: 0-328-15690-6 (D)

3 4 5 6 7 8 9 10 V063 12 11 10 09 08 07 06 05

Consulting Author

Dr. Michael P. Klentschy
Superintendent
El Centro Elementary School District
El Centro, California

Science Content Consultants

Dr. Frederick W. Taylor
Senior Research Scientist
Institute for Geophysics
Jackson School of Geosciences
The University of Texas at Austin
Austin, Texas

Dr. Ruth E. Buskirk
Senior Lecturer
School of Biological Sciences
The University of Texas at Austin
Austin, Texas

Dr. Cliff Frohlich
Senior Research Scientist
Institute for Geophysics
Jackson School of Geosciences
The University of Texas at Austin
Austin, Texas

Brad Armosky
McDonald Observatory
The University of Texas at Austin
Austin, Texas

NASA Content Consultants

Adena Williams Loston, Ph.D.
Chief Education Officer
Office of the Chief Education Officer

Clifford W. Houston, Ph.D.
Deputy Chief Education Officer for Education Programs
Office of the Chief Education Officer

Frank C. Owens
Senior Policy Advisor
Office of the Chief Education Officer

Deborah Brown Biggs
Manager, Education Flight Projects Office
Space Operations Mission Directorate, Education Lead

Erika G. Vick
NASA Liaison to Pearson Scott Foresman
Education Flight Projects Office

William E. Anderson
Partnership Manager for Education
Aeronautics Research Mission Directorate

Anita Krishnamurthi
Program Planning Specialist
Space Science Education and Outreach Program

Bonnie J. McClain
Chief of Education
Exploration Systems Mission Directorate

Diane Schweizer
Program Scientist
Earth Science Education

Deborah Rivera
Strategic Alliances Manager
Office of Public Affairs
NASA Headquarters

Douglas D. Peterson
Public Affairs Officer, Astronaut Office
Office of Public Affairs
NASA Johnson Space Center

Nicole Cloutier
Public Affairs Officer, Astronaut Office
Office of Public Affairs
NASA Johnson Space Center

Dr. Jennifer J. Wiseman
Hubble Space Scientist Program Scientist
NASA Headquarters

Reviewers

Science

See learning in a whole new light

How to Read Science xx

Science Process Skills xxii

Using Scientific Methods xxvi

Science Tools xxviii

Safety in Science xxxii

Unit A Life Science

How do plants live in their habitats?

Chapter 1 • All About Plants

Build Background How do plants live in their habitats? . . . 2

Lab zone **Directed Inquiry Explore** Do plants need water? . . 4

How to Read Science Predict 5

Chapter 1 Song "Plants" 6

Lesson 1 • What are the parts of a plant? 7

Lesson 2 • How are seeds scattered? 10

Lesson 3 • How are plants grouped? 12

Lesson 4 • How are some woodland plants adapted?. . 16

Lesson 5 • How are some prairie plants adapted? . . . 20

Lesson 6 • How are some desert plants adapted? . . . 22

Lesson 7 • How are some marsh plants adapted? . . . 24

Lab zone **Guided Inquiry Investigate** Do plants need light?. 26

Math in Science Leaf Patterns 28

Chapter 1 Review and Test Prep. 30

Biography Mary Agnes Chase 32

Chapter 2 • All About Animals

How are animals different from each other?

Build Background How are animals different from each other?. 34

Directed Inquiry Explore How are worms and snakes alike and different? 36

How to Read Science Alike and Different . . . 37

Chapter 2 Song "What Has Backbones?" 38

Lesson 1 • What are some animals with backbones?. . 39

Lesson 2 • What are some ways mammals are adapted? 42

Lesson 3 • What are some ways birds are adapted? . . 44

Lesson 4 • What are some ways fish are adapted?. . . 46

Lesson 5 • What are some ways reptiles are adapted? . 48

Lesson 6 • What are some ways amphibians are adapted? 50

Lesson 7 • What are some animals without backbones? 52

Guided Inquiry Investigate How can an octopus use its arms? 56

Math in Science Sorting Animals. 58

Chapter 2 Review and Test Prep 60

NASA Life Along the Ice. 62

Career Wildlife Rehabilitator 64

Unit A Life Science

How do living things help each other?

Chapter 3 • How Plants and Animals Live Together

Build Background How do living things help each other? 66

Lab zone Directed Inquiry Explore What does yeast need to grow? 68

How to Read Science Cause and Effect 69

Chapter 3 Song "Good Partners" 70

Lesson 1 • What do plants and animals need? 71

Lesson 2 • How do plants and animals get food in a grassland? 74

Lesson 3 • How do plants and animals get food in an ocean? 78

Lesson 4 • What can cause a food web to change? . . 82

Lesson 5 • How do plants and animals help each other? 84

Lab zone Guided Inquiry Investigate How can you make a model of a food web? 90

Math in Science Measuring Length 92

Chapter 3 Review and Test Prep 94

Career Farmer 96

Chapter 4 • How Living Things Grow and Change

Build Background How do living things grow in different ways? 98

Lab zone **Directed Inquiry Explore** Which hand do different children use to write? 100

How to Read Science Infer 101

Chapter 4 Song "Hi Little Turtle!" 102

Lesson 1 • How do sea turtles grow and change? . . 103

Lesson 2 • What is the life cycle of a dragonfly? . . . 108

Lesson 3 • What is the life cycle of a horse? 110

Lesson 4 • How are young animals like their parents? 112

Lesson 5 • What is the life cycle of a bean plant? . . 114

Lesson 6 • How are young plants like their parents? . 116

Lesson 7 • How do people grow and change? 118

Lab zone **Guided Activity Investigate** How does a caterpillar grow and change? 122

Math in Science Measuring Time. 124

Chapter 4 Review and Test Prep 126

NASA **Biography** Mario Mota 128

Unit A Test Talk 129

Unit A Wrap-Up 130

Lab zone **Full Inquiry Experiment** Which bird beak can crush seeds? 132

End with a Poem "Little Seeds" 134

Science Fair Projects: Temperature and Seeds; Jumping Insects. 136

How do living things grow in different ways?

Unit B Earth Science

What are Earth's natural resources?

Chapter 5 • Earth's Land, Air, and Water

Build Background What are Earth's natural resources? . . 138

Lab zone Directed Inquiry Explore How are soils different? 140

How to Read Science Picture Clues 141

Chapter 5 Song "Natural Resources" 142

Lesson 1 • What are natural resources? 143

Lesson 2 • What are rocks and soil like? 146

Lesson 3 • How do people use plants? 150

Lesson 4 • How does Earth change? 152

Lesson 5 • How can people help protect Earth? . . . 154

Lab zone Guided Inquiry Investigate How do worms change the soil? 160

Math in Science Recycling Bar Graph 162

Chapter 5 Review and Test Prep 164

NASA Looking out for Earth 166

Career Forester 168

Chapter 6 • Earth's Weather and Seasons

Build Background How does weather change? 170

Lab zone **Directed Inquiry Explore** How much rain falls? . 172

How to Read Science Draw Conclusions . . . 173

Chapter 6 Song "What's the Weather?" 174

Lesson 1 • What are some kinds of weather? 175

Lesson 2 • What is the water cycle? 178

Lesson 3 • What is spring? 180

Lesson 4 • What is summer? 182

Lesson 5 • What is fall? 184

Lesson 6 • What is winter? 186

Lesson 7 • What are some kinds of bad weather? . . 188

Lab zone **Guided Inquiry Investigate** How can you measure weather changes? 194

Math in Science Charting Favorite Seasons. 196

Chapter 6 Review and Test Prep 198

Career Atmospheric Scientist 200

How does weather change?

Unit B Earth Science

How can people learn about the Earth long ago?

Chapter 7 • Fossils and Dinosaurs

Build Background How can people learn about Earth long ago? 202

Directed Inquiry Explore Which fossils match the plants and animals? 204

How to Read Science Retell 205

Chapter 7 Song "Go Find A Fossil" 206

Lesson 1 • How can we learn about the past? 207

Lesson 2 • What can we learn from fossils? 210

Lesson 3 • What were dinosaurs like? 212

Lesson 4 • What are some new discoveries? 216

Guided Inquiry Investigate How can you make a model of a fossil? 218

Math in Science Measuring Fossil Leaves 220

Chapter 7 Review and Test Prep 222

Biography Susan Hendrickson 224

Unit B Test Talk 225

Unit B Wrap-Up 226

Full Inquiry Experiment Where would you look for the best fossils? 228

End with a Poem "The Spring Wind" 230

Science Fair Projects: Water Evaporates; Measuring Temperature 232

Unit C · Physical Science

What are some properties of matter?

Chapter 8 • Properties of Matter

Build Background What are some properties of matter? . 234

Lab zone Directed Inquiry Explore What happens when oil is mixed with water? 236

How to Read Science Draw Conclusions . . . 237

Chapter 8 Song "They're All Matter" 238

Lesson 1 • What is matter? 239

Lesson 2 • What are the states of matter? 242

Lesson 3 • How can matter be changed? 248

Lesson 4 • How can cooling and heating change matter? 252

Lab zone Guided Inquiry Investigate How can water change? 256

Math in Science How Can You Measure Matter? . . . 258

Chapter 8 Review and Test Prep 260

NASA Space Food 262

NASA Career Material Scientist 264

Chapter 9 • Energy

Build Background What are some kinds of energy? . . . 266

Lab zone **Directed Inquiry Explore** Which color heats faster? 268

How to Read Science Infer 269

Chapter 9 Song "Where Do We Get Energy?" 270

Lesson 1 • What is energy? 271

Lesson 2 • How do living things use energy? 274

Lesson 3 • What are some sources of heat? 278

Lesson 4 • How does light move? 282

Lesson 5 • What are other kinds of energy? 286

Lab zone **Guided Inquiry Investigate** How can you change light? 290

Math in Science Measuring Shadows 292

Chapter 9 Review and Test Prep 294

Career Lighting Operator 296

What are some kinds of energy?

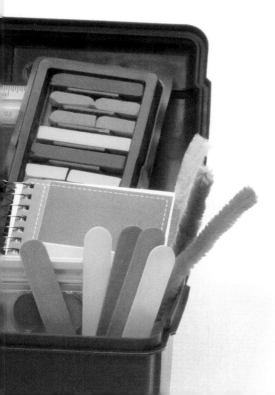

Unit C Physical Science

How do forces cause objects to move?

Chapter 10 • Forces and Motion

Build Background How do forces cause objects to move? 298

Directed Inquiry Explore How can you measure force?. 300

How to Read Science Put Things in Order. . 301

Chapter 10 Song "Use Some Force!" 302

Lesson 1 • How do objects move?. 303

Lesson 2 • What is work?. 308

Lesson 3 • How can you change the way things move? 310

Lesson 4 • How can simple machines help you do work? 314

Lesson 5 • What are magnets? 318

Guided Inquiry Investigate What can magnets do? 322

Math in Science Measuring Motion 324

Chapter 10 Review and Test Prep 326

Biography Luther Jenkins 328

Chapter 11 • Sound

Build Background How is sound made?. 330

Lab zone **Directed Inquiry Explore** How can you make sound? 332

How to Read Science Important Details . . . 333

Chapter 11 Song "Listen to the Sounds!" 334

Lesson 1 • What is sound? 335

Lesson 2 • What is pitch? 338

Lesson 3 • How does sound travel? 340

Lesson 4 • How do some animals make sounds? . . . 342

Lesson 5 • What are some sounds around you? . . . 344

Lab zone **Guided Inquiry Investigate** How can you change sound? 346

Math in Science Measuring Sounds 348

Chapter 11 Review and Test Prep 350

Biography Alejandro Purgue 352

Unit C Test Talk 353

Unit C Wrap-Up 354

Lab zone **Full Inquiry Experiment** What kinds of objects reflect light clearly? 356

End with a Poem "Apple Shadows" 358

Science Fair Projects: Energy in My Terrarium; Listening to Sound Through Matter. 360

How is sound made?

Unit D Space and Technology

What are some ways the Earth moves?

Chapter 12 • Earth and Space

Build Background What are some ways the Earth moves? 362

Lab zone **Directed Inquiry Explore** What causes day and night? 364

How to Read Science Alike and Different . . 365

Chapter 12 Song "The Sun" 366

Lesson 1 • What is the Sun? 367

Lesson 2 • What causes day and night? 370

Lesson 3 • What causes seasons to change? 374

Lesson 4 • What can you see in the night sky? 376

Lesson 5 • Why does the moon seem to change? . . . 380

Lesson 6 • What is the solar system? 382

Lab zone **Guided Inquiry Investigate** How can you make a model of a constellation? 384

Math in Science Planets in Orbit 386

Chapter 12 Review and Test Prep 388

NASA Mission to Mars 390

NASA **Career** Astronomer 392

Chapter 13 • Technology in Our World

Build Background What are some ways technology helps us? 394

Lab zone **Directed Inquiry Explore** How can you move the ball? 396

How to Read Science Retell 397

Chapter 13 Song "Technology Helps Us All" 398

Lesson 1 • What is technology? 399

Lesson 2 • How does technology help us? 402

Lesson 3 • How do we use technology to communicate? 404

Lesson 4 • What are some other ways we use technology? 406

Lesson 5 • How do people make things? 408

Lab zone **Guided Inquiry Investigate** How can you make a maze? 410

Math in Science Technology in Your School 412

Chapter 13 Review and Test Prep 414

Biography Shonte Wright 416

Unit D Test Talk 417

Unit D Wrap-Up 418

Lab zone **Full Inquiry Experiment** Which tissue is the strongest? 420

End with a Poem "This Happy Day" 422

Science Fair Projects: Phases of the Moon; Flying Better 424

Metric and Customary Measurements EM1

Glossary EM2

Index EM22

Credits . . . . EM 30

What are some ways technology helps us?

How to Read Science

Each chapter in your book has a page like this one. This page shows you how to use a reading skill.

Before reading

First, read the Build Background page. Next, read the How To Read Science page. Then, think about what you already know. Last, make a list of what you already know.

Target Reading Skill

Each page has a target reading skill. The target reading skill will help you understand what you read.

Real-World Connection

Each page has an example of something you will learn.

Graphic Organizer

A graphic organizer can help you think about what you learn.

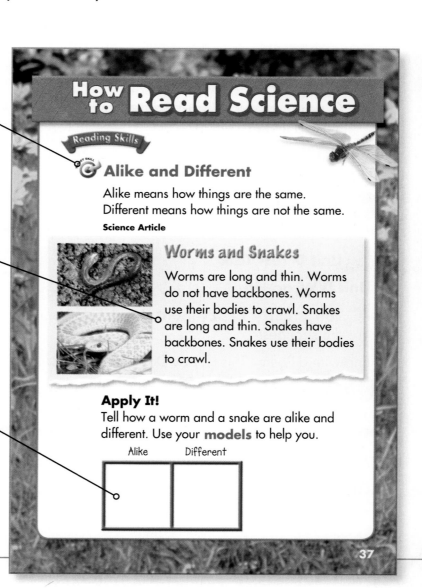

How to Read Science

Reading Skills

Alike and Different

Alike means how things are the same. Different means how things are not the same.

Science Article

Worms and Snakes

Worms are long and thin. Worms do not have backbones. Worms use their bodies to crawl. Snakes are long and thin. Snakes have backbones. Snakes use their bodies to crawl.

Apply It!

Tell how a worm and a snake are alike and different. Use your **models** to help you.

Alike	Different

37

Reptiles are animals with backbones. Most reptiles have dry skin. Scales cover and protect a reptile's body. Some reptiles hatch from eggs. Snakes and turtles are two kinds of reptiles. Look at the picture of the reptile.

Amphibians are animals with backbones. Amphibians live part of their life in the water and part of their life on land. Most amphibians have smooth, wet skin. Amphibians hatch from eggs. Frogs and toads are amphibians.

✓**Lesson Checkpoint**

1. Which kinds of animals have backbones and scales?

2. 🎯 How are an amphibian and a reptile **alike** and **different?**

amphibian

reptile

41

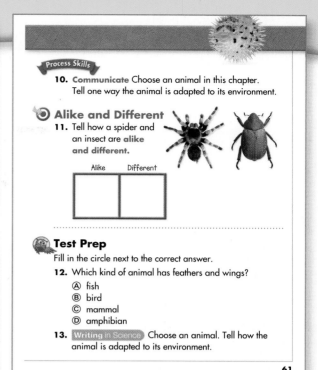

Process Skills

10. **Communicate** Choose an animal in this chapter. Tell one way the animal is adapted to its environment.

🎯 **Alike and Different**

11. Tell how a spider and an insect are **alike and different.**

Alike	Different

Test Prep

Fill in the circle next to the correct answer.

12. Which kind of animal has feathers and wings?
    Ⓐ fish
    Ⓑ bird
    Ⓒ mammal
    Ⓓ amphibian

13. Writing in Science Choose an animal. Tell how the animal is adapted to its environment.

61

During reading

Use the checkpoint as you read the lesson. This will help you check how much you understand.

After reading

Think about what you have learned. Compare what you learned with the list you made before you read the chapter. Answer the questions in the Chapter Review.

Target Reading Skills

These are some target reading skills that appear in this book.

- Cause and Effect
- Alike and Different
- Put Things in Order
- Predict

- Draw Conclusions
- Picture Clues
- Important Details

Science Process Skills

Observe

A scientist who wants to find out more about space observes many things. You use your senses to find out about things too.

Classify

Scientists classify objects in space. You classify when you sort or group things by their properties.

Estimate and Measure

Scientists build machines to explore space. First scientists make a careful guess about the size or amount of the parts of the machine. Then they measure each part.

Infer

Scientists are always learning about space. Scientists draw a conclusion or make a guess from what they already know.

Scientists use process skills to find out about things. You will use these skills when you do the activities in this book. Suppose scientists want to learn more about space. Which process skills might they use?

Space

Predict

First scientists tell what they think will happen. Then they do an experiment.

Make and Use Models

Scientists might make and use models of a machine to use in space. Models show what scientists already know.

Make Definitions

Scientists use what they know to tell what something means.

Science Process Skills

Suppose you were a scientist. You might want to learn more about space. What questions might you have? How would you use process skills to help you learn?

Make Hypotheses

Think of a question you have about space. Make a statement that you can test to answer your question.

Collect Data

Scientists record what they observe and measure. Scientists put this data into charts or graphs.

Interpret Data

Scientists use what they learn to solve problems or answer questions.

Unit D

Space and Technology

You Will Discover

- what is in the day and night sky.
- how Earth, the Sun, and the Moon move.

Chapter 12
Earth and Space

Discovery Channel School
Student DVD

online
Student Edition
sfsuccessnet.com

What are some ways the Earth moves?

solar system

rotation   axis

constellation

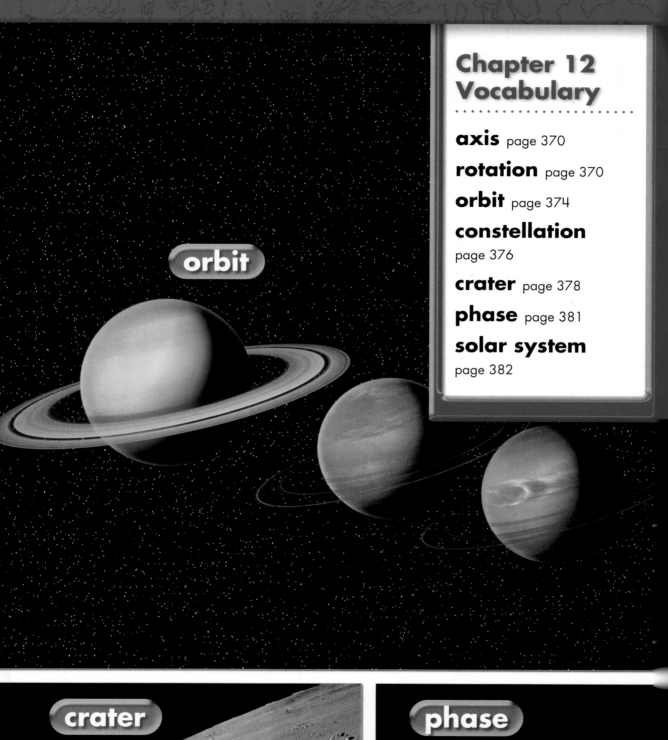

orbit

Chapter 12 Vocabulary

axis page 370

rotation page 370

orbit page 374

constellation page 376

crater page 378

phase page 381

solar system page 382

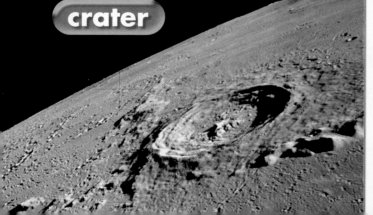

crater

phase

Explore What causes day and night?

Materials

foam ball

pencil

dot sticker

crayons or markers

flashlight

What to Do

1 **Make a model** of Earth.

foam ball

red dot sticker

child

2 Shine a flashlight on your model.

The flashlight is like the Sun.

Process Skills

You can use **models** of Earth and the Sun to understand what causes day and night.

3 Turn your model of Earth. Watch the child.

Explain Your Results

How does your **model** show day and night?

How to Read Science

 Alike and Different

Alike means how things are the same.
Different means how things are not the same.

Science Pictures

Day and Night

Apply It!
Look at the pictures.
Tell how day and night
are alike and different.
Think of your **model**
to help you.

Alike	Different

The Sun

Sung to the tune of "Twinkle Twinkle Little Star"
Lyrics by Gerri Brioso & Richard Freitas/The Dovetail Group, Inc.

In the sky's a great big star.
It's the Sun and it's real far!
The Sun lights up the sky so bright.
It also lights the Moon at night.
Heat and light come from the sun
And that is needed by everyone!

Lesson 1
What is the Sun?

Think of the stars you see in the sky at night. Stars are made of hot, glowing gases. The Sun is a star too. The Sun seems brighter and larger than the other stars. This is because the Sun is the closest star to Earth. The Sun is so bright that you cannot see other stars during the day.

Why We Need the Sun

The Sun may look small, but it is really very big. The Sun is much bigger than Earth. The Sun looks small because it is so far away.

This is what the Sun looks like in space.

The Sun is important to Earth. Earth gets light and heat from the Sun. Living things on Earth need light and heat. People, plants, and animals can live on Earth because of the Sun.

✓ **Lesson Checkpoint**

1. Why is the Sun important to living things on Earth?

2. How are the Sun and other stars **alike** and **different?**

Lesson 2

What causes day and night?

The picture shows an imaginary line through the center of Earth. This line is called an **axis.** Earth is always spinning on its axis. This spinning on an axis is called a **rotation.** Earth makes one complete rotation each day.

Earth's rotation causes day and night. When your side of Earth is facing the Sun, you have day. When your side of Earth is facing away from the Sun, you have night.

✓ Checkpoint

1. What is Earth's axis?

2. Writing in Science Write 2 sentences in your **science journal.** Tell why one side of Earth has day when the other side has night.

It takes about 24 hours for Earth to make one complete rotation.

Lesson 3

What causes seasons to change?

The pictures show that Earth is tilted on its axis. Earth is always tilted in the same direction.

You know that Earth spins on its axis. Earth also moves around the Sun in an orbit. An **orbit** is a path around another object. It takes Earth about one year to orbit the Sun one time. The tilt of Earth and Earth's orbit around the Sun cause the seasons to change.

✓ **Lesson Checkpoint**

1. What causes the seasons to change?

2. **Social Studies** in Science Look at a calendar. When is the official first day of summer?

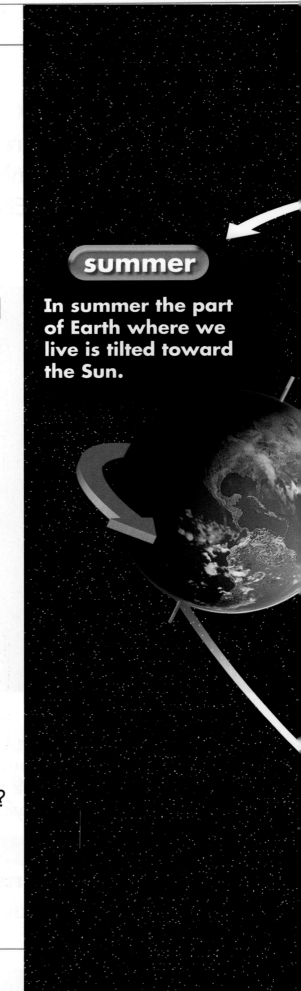

summer

In summer the part of Earth where we live is tilted toward the Sun.

374

spring

In spring the part of the Earth where we live is beginning to tilt toward the Sun.

summer

In summer the part of Earth where we live is tilted toward the Sun.

winter

In winter the part of Earth where we live is tilted away from the Sun.

fall

In fall the part of Earth where we live is beginning to tilt away from the Sun.

The Moon

You might see the Moon in the night sky too. The Moon is the largest and brightest object in the night sky.

The Moon has mountains and deep craters. A **crater** is a hole in the ground that is shaped like a bowl. A crater is formed when a large rock from space hits the Moon.

Look at the chart.

1. Which of these planets takes the most number of days to orbit the Sun?

2. Which of these planets takes the fewest number of days to orbit the Sun?

3. List these planets in order from the fewest to the most number of days to orbit the Sun.

Uranus

Pluto

Neptune

Saturn

Vocabulary
Which picture goes with each word?

1. axis
2. crater
3. constellation
4. orbit
5. phase
6. rotation
7. solar system

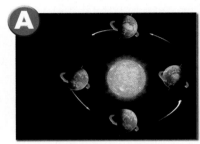

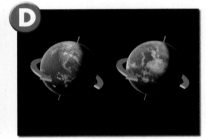

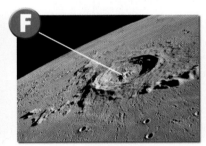

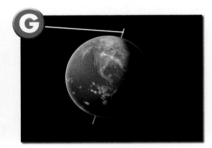

What did you learn?

8. What is caused by Earth's rotation?
9. Why is the Sun the only star you can see during the day?

10. Communicate Tell why we have light during the day.

Alike and Different

11. Tell how the Sun and the Moon
are **alike** and **different.**

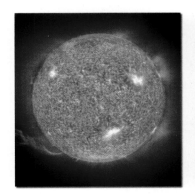 

Alike	Different

Test Prep

Fill in the circle next to the correct answer.

12. Which star is closest to Earth?

Ⓐ the Sun

Ⓑ the Big Dipper

Ⓒ the Moon

Ⓓ Leo

13. **Writing** in Science Describe what you might
see if you traveled around the solar system.

Mission To Mars

NASA scientists want to learn more about the planet Mars. Mars is a planet that is close to Earth. Mars and Earth are alike in some ways. Water is needed for life on Earth. Scientists want to learn more about water on Mars.

NASA sent robots to Mars to learn about the planet. Some robots fly around Mars taking pictures. Some robots called rovers have landed on Mars. These rovers travel across the surface.

Scientists use the robots to study the environment on Mars. They take pictures of the soil and the rocks on Mars. Rovers also dig into the ground.

This rover is called *Opportunity. Opportunity* landed in a place called **Meridiani Planum.**

Lab zone **Take-Home Activity**

Suppose you are a scientist studying Mars. Write a question that you have about Mars.

Astronomer

Laura Peticolas is an astronomer who works with NASA. She studies natural displays of light called *auroras.* Two examples of auroras are Northern lights and Southern lights.

Read Together

Have you ever looked at the stars at night? People who study the Sun, stars, planets, and other things far from Earth are called astronomers.

Many astronomers use special tools called telescopes to help them see far out into space. A telescope helps things that are far away look nearer, larger and brighter.

To study the universe, scientists at NASA launch many telescopes. One such telescope is the Hubble Space Telescope. Every day this telescope sends information to astronomers all over the world.

Lab zone Take-Home Activity

Go outside on a clear night with your family. Look at the sky. Write about what you see.

You Will Discover
- how technology has changed the world we live in.
- ways we use technology every day.

Chapter 13
Technology in Our World

online
Student Edition
sfsuccessnet.com

What are some ways technology helps us?

technology

engine

vaccine

Vaccine

satellite

394

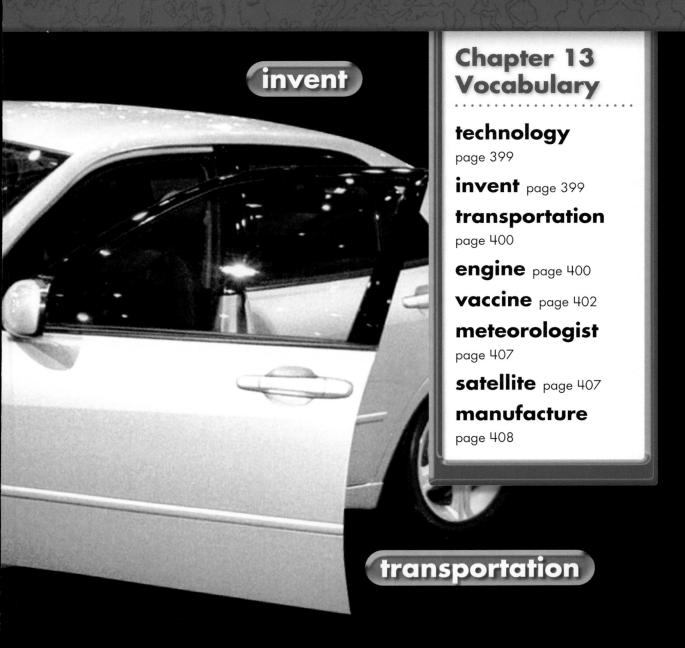

invent

Chapter 13 Vocabulary

technology
page 399

invent page 399

transportation
page 400

engine page 400

vaccine page 402

meteorologist
page 407

satellite page 407

manufacture
page 408

transportation

manufacture

To make by hand or machine.

meteorologist

Explore How can you move the ball?

Materials

metal ball

books

cup

pencil

ruler

magnet

spoon

What to Do

1 Put the ball on the books.
Place the cup 25 cm away
from the books.

2 Solve this problem.
Put the ball in the cup.
Use tools.

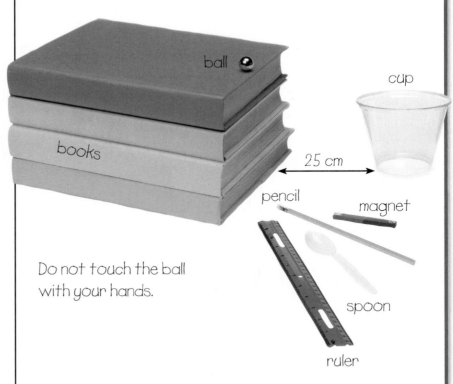

ball

books

25 cm

cup

pencil

magnet

spoon

ruler

*Do not touch the ball
with your hands.*

Process Skills

When you
communicate,
you tell how you
moved the ball.

Explain Your Results

Communicate Tell how
you solved the problem.

Reading Skills

TARGET SKILL

Retell

Retell means to tell what you learned in your own words.

Science Article

Bicycles

The first bicycle was invented in 1817. Riders pushed their feet on the ground to make it move. Pedals were added in 1839. The pedals helped people ride bicycles with their feet off the ground.

Apply It!

Communicate

Tell what you learned about bicycles.

Retell

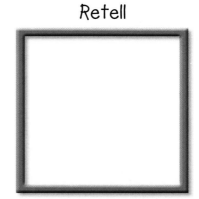

Technology Helps Us All

Sung to the tune of "Bingo"
Lyrics by Gerri Brioso & Richard Freitas/The Dovetail Group, Inc.

Technology now helps us all
In lots of different ways. It
Helps us travel fast,
Helps us travel far,
Helps us travel safe,
In cars, and trains and airplanes.

Lesson 1

What is technology?

Every day people ride in cars. People use cell phones and computers. We can do these things because of technology. **Technology** means using science to help us solve problems.

Sometimes people use technology to invent things. **Invent** means to make something for the first time.

Inventions can be things we need or things we want. We need cars and airplanes to help us travel long distances. Computer games are things we want.

SciLinks Take It to the Net
sfsuccessnet.com   keyword: technology
code: g2p399

399

Changes in Transportation

Technology has changed transportation. **Transportation** is the way people or things move from place to place. Today people travel farther and faster than they did long ago.

Some kinds of transportation have engines. An **engine** is a machine that does work or makes something move. Long ago, steam engines were used to make trains and boats move. Today, cars, trains, and boats have gasoline or electric engines.

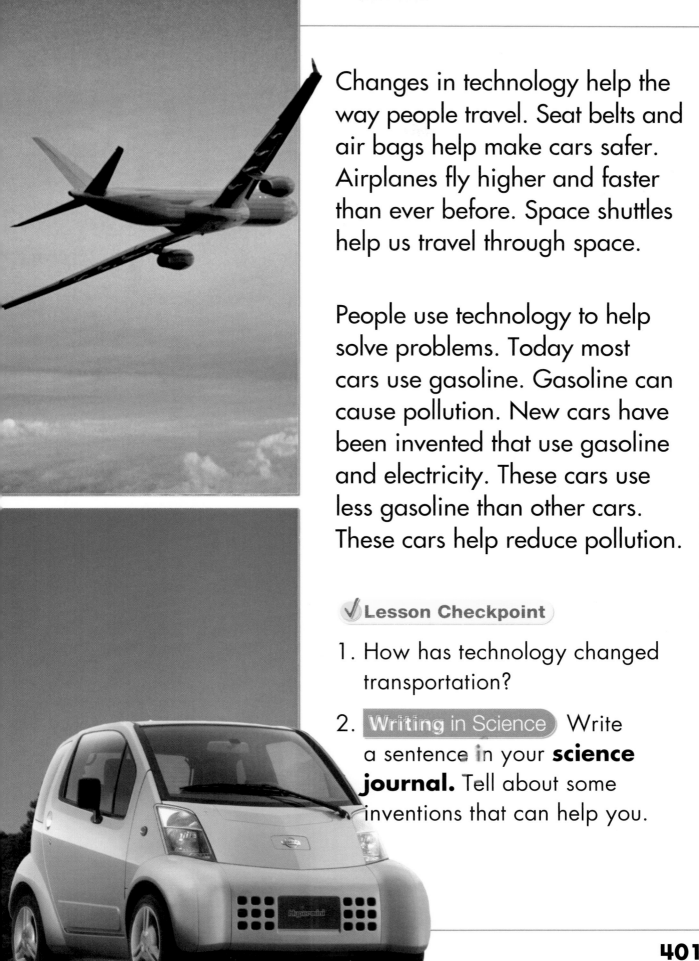

Changes in technology help the way people travel. Seat belts and air bags help make cars safer. Airplanes fly higher and faster than ever before. Space shuttles help us travel through space.

People use technology to help solve problems. Today most cars use gasoline. Gasoline can cause pollution. New cars have been invented that use gasoline and electricity. These cars use less gasoline than other cars. These cars help reduce pollution.

✓ **Lesson Checkpoint**

1. How has technology changed transportation?

2. **Writing in Science** Write a sentence in your **science journal.** Tell about some inventions that can help you.

Lesson 2

How does technology help us?

Technology can help people stay healthy. Doctors use technology to make vaccines to help prevent people from getting sick. A **vaccine** is a medicine that can help prevent a disease.

vaccine

Doctors use technology to help people in many ways. Glasses and contact lenses can help people who have trouble seeing. Hearing aids can help people who have trouble hearing. Artificial legs can help some people to walk.

The doctor uses an x-ray to help this boy get well.

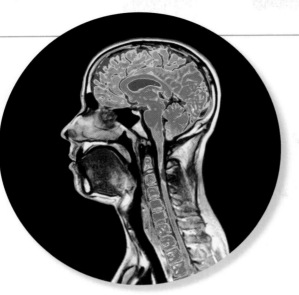

This is a picture from an MRI.

Technology can help doctors find out why people are sick. X-rays, CAT scans, and MRIs are tools doctors can use to see inside people. When doctors know what is wrong, they can help people to get well.

This man can run with the help of his artificial leg.

✓ Lesson Checkpoint

1. What are some ways that technology can help people?

2. **Retell** What are some tools that help doctors see inside people?

Lesson 3

How do we use technology to communicate?

What are some ways you communicate with your friends? You might make a phone call. You might send an instant message from your computer. The way technology is used to communicate has changed over the years.

Long ago, telephones were attached to a wall. Today you can carry a telephone with you. Telephones are much smaller and lighter today than they were years ago.

This telephone is from 1879!

Early computers were very big and very heavy. Long ago only a few large companies used computers. Today computers can be found in many places. Today computers are smaller, faster, and easier to use than early computers.

The first computer was invented in 1946. It filled a whole room!

Technology helps us communicate with astronauts in space. Astronauts can now use computers to send messages from space.

✓ Lesson Checkpoint

1. How has technology changed the way people communicate?

2. **Math** in Science An area code in Miami, Florida, is 305. An area code in Chicago, Illinois, is 312. Add the area codes together.

Lesson 4

What are some other ways we use technology?

Technology has changed the way people have fun. People listen to music on compact discs. People use computers to play games.

Technology can also make our lives easier. People use velcro to close things. People use calculators to do math.

MP3 players play music.

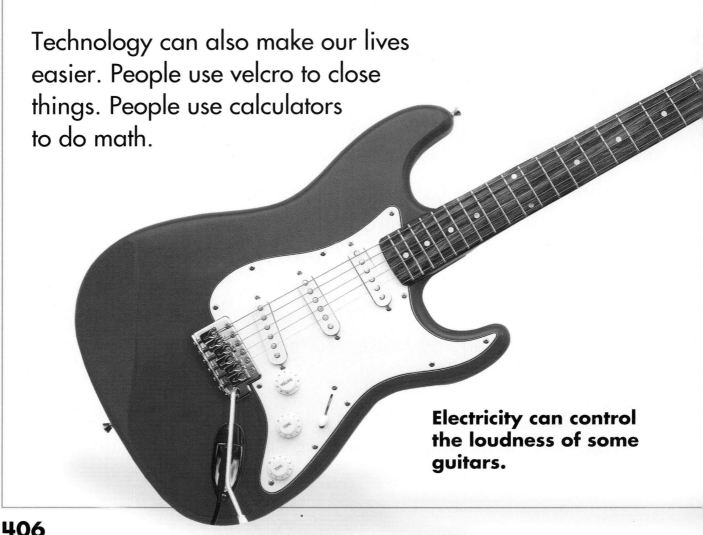

Electricity can control the loudness of some guitars.

Technology helps people in their jobs. A **meteorologist** is a person who studies weather. Meteorologists get information about the weather from satellites. A **satellite** is an object that revolves around another object. Satellites in space send pictures back to Earth. Meteorologists use the pictures to tell us what the weather will be like.

Satellites like this one send information about the weather to Earth.

√ **Lesson Checkpoint**

1. How does a meteorologist use information from satellites?

2. **Writing** in Science Write a sentence in your **science journal.** Tell three ways you used technology today.

How do people make things?

People manufacture things we use every day. **Manufacture** means to make by hand or by machines. Coats and bicycles are two things that are manufactured.

Natural materials were used to make parts of this coat.

Different types of materials are used to manufacture things. Some materials come from nature. This coat was made using wool from sheep. The buttons were made from wood.

Some materials are made by people. The seat of this bicycle is made from plastic. The tires are made from rubber. Plastic and rubber are materials made by people.

This bike uses materials made by people.

√ **Lesson Checkpoint**

1. What are some manufactured things you use in school?

2. **Retell** What are some materials used to make a bicycle?

Investigate How can you make a maze?

Materials

safety goggles

marble

cardboard

paper tubes

box

tape and scissors

Process Skills

You **predict** when you tell what you think will happen.

What to Do

1 How can you make a maze that a marble can follow? Make a plan. Draw it.

2 Tape paper tubes to the cardboard.

3 **Predict** Will your maze work?

4 Test your maze. **Observe** the marble. Move the tubes to make the maze work better.

5 Test your maze 2 more times.

Test your maze.	
Test	**Did the marble follow the maze?**
1	
2	
3	

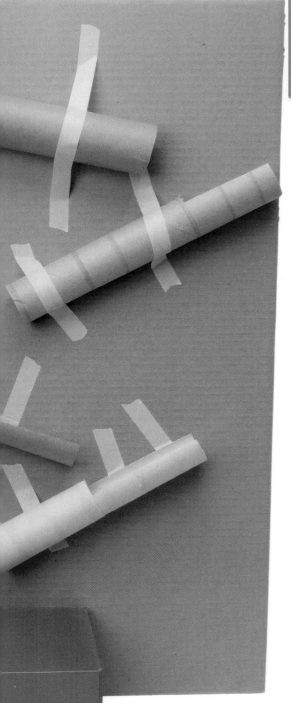

Your maze might look like this one.

Be sure to wear your safety goggles.

Explain Your Results

Communicate Tell how the parts of your maze work together.

Go Further

How can you make your marble move in a different way? Investigate to find out.

Technology in Your School

Look around your school. How many things can you find that help people communicate? How many things can you find that help people move from place to place? Fill in your table with examples.

Technology in My School

Communication	Transportation

1. Count the examples you found for each column.
2. Compare the number of examples you found. Use <, >, or =.

Lab zone **Take-Home Activity**

Walk around your home. Look for ways you use technology. Make a table like the one you made for your school.

413

Vocabulary

Which picture goes with each word?

1. engine
2. vaccine
3. satellite
4. meteorologist

A

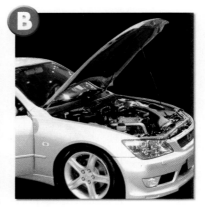

B

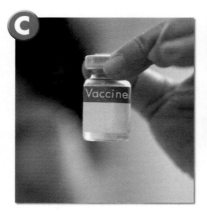

C

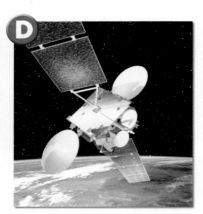

D

What did you learn?

5. What is technology?

6. Name two ways you use technology every day.

7. How has technology changed communication?

8. **Infer** Why do people invent new things?

Retell

9. Tell what you learned about toothbrushes.

Retell

The first toothbrush was invented in China in the 1400s. The bristles were made from animal hair. The first electric toothbrush was invented in 1960. Today, bristles are made from nylon.

Test Prep

Fill in the circle next to the correct answer.

10. What is an object that travels around another object?

Ⓐ engine

Ⓑ vaccine

Ⓒ satellite

Ⓓ velcro

11. **Writing in Science** Make a list. Tell how people use technology.

Meet Shonte Wright

Shonte Wright traveled across the United States with five other scientists. They told people about the rovers that landed on Mars in 2004.

Read Together

In 2004 NASA sent two robots to Mars. The robots were called rovers. The rovers took pictures of Mars and sent them back to Earth. NASA used the pictures to study the planet.

Shonte Wright is one of the scientists who worked with NASA on the rovers. She helped make sure the rovers would still work after the long trip through space.

Ms. Wright knew she wanted to be a scientist and work at NASA when she was ten years old. She took many math and science classes to help her get ready for her job.

Lab zone Take-Home Activity

Suppose you are going to invent a robot to explore another planet. Draw what the robot would look like.

Unit D Test Talk

Test-Taking Strategies

Find Important Words
Choose the Right Answer
Use Information from Text and Graphics
▶ Write Your Answer

Write Your Answer

You can write your answer to science questions. Remember that your answer should be short but complete.

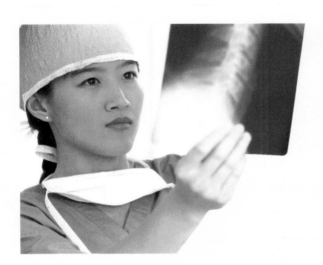

Doctors use technology to help you when you are sick or hurt. They can use X-ray, CAT scan, or an MRI to see inside your body. Best of all, using these machines doesn't hurt!

Read the question. Look at the text.

1. Why does a doctor use X-ray or CAT scan technology?

Which words can you use to help write your answer? Write your answer.

Unit D Wrap-Up

Chapter 12

What are some ways the Earth moves?
- Earth is always spinning on its axis.
- Earth moves around the Sun in an orbit.

Chapter 13

What are some ways technology helps us?
- Technology helps people travel, communicate, and make things.
- Doctors use technology to help people get well.

Performance Assessment

Make a Technology Collage

- Find pictures of people using technology to communicate.
- Cut out the pictures.
- Make a collage.
- Tell about the pictures you found.

Read More About Space & Technology!

Look for books like these in your library.

Lab zone Full Inquiry

Experiment Which tissue is the strongest?

Tissues can be strong or weak. Experiment to find out which tissue is the strongest. The tissue that holds the most water is the strongest.

Materials

3 tissues

jar and rubber band

dropper and cup with water

marbles

balance

gram cubes

Process Skills

You **collect data** when you use a chart to record your data.

Ask a question.

Are tissues that cost more stronger than tissues that cost less?

Make a hypothesis.

If a tissue costs the most, then it is the strongest.

Plan a fair test.

Use the same amount of water to wet each tissue. Use 3 different brands of tissue.

Do your test.

1 Put a tissue on the jar. Put a rubber band around it.

2 Wet the tissue drop by drop. Use 30 drops.

More Lab zone Activities Take It to the Net
sfsuccessnet.com

3 Carefully place one marble at a time on top of the tissue.

4 Count how many marbles it takes to break the tissue.

5 **Measure** the mass of the marbles.

6 Repeat with the other tissues.

Collect and record data.

Tissue Cost	How many marbles?	How many grams?
Most		
Middle		
Least		

Tell your conclusion.
Which tissue is the strongest?

Go Further
What if you used less water to wet each tissue? Try it and find out.

This Happy Day

by Harry Behn

Every morning when the sun
Comes smiling up on everyone,
It's lots of fun
To say good morning to the sun.
Good morning, Sun!

Every evening after play
When the sunshine goes away,
It's nice to say,
Thank you for this happy day,
This happy day!

Full Inquiry

Using Scientific Methods

1. Ask a question.
2. Make a hypothesis.
3. Plan a Fair Test.
4. Do Your Test.
5. Collect and record data.
6. Tell Your Conclusion.
7. Go further.

Idea 1

Phases of the Moon

Plan a project. Find out what the Moon looks like every day for one month.

Idea 2

Flying Better

Make a plan. Find out if changing the size of a helicopter's blades will make it fly better.

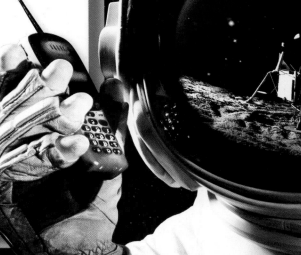

Metric and Customary Measures

Science uses the metric system to measure things. Metric measurement is used around the world. Here is how different metric measurements compare to customary measurement.

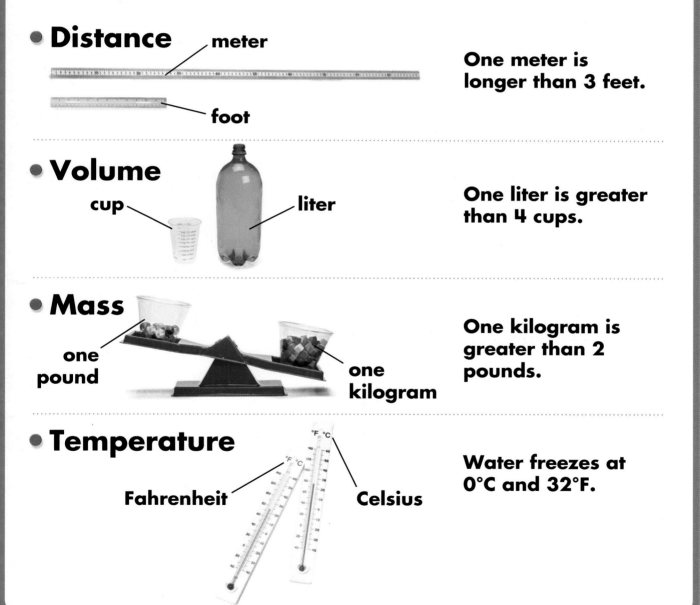

- **Distance**

  meter

  foot

  One meter is longer than 3 feet.

- **Volume**

  cup

  liter

  One liter is greater than 4 cups.

- **Mass**

  one pound

  one kilogram

  One kilogram is greater than 2 pounds.

- **Temperature**

  Fahrenheit

  Celsius

  Water freezes at 0°C and 32°F.

Glossary

The glossary uses letters and signs to show how words are pronounced. The mark ′ is placed after a syllable with a primary or heavy accent. The mark ′ is placed after a syllable with a secondary or lighter accent.

To hear these words pronounced, listen to the AudioText CD.

A

adapt (ə dapt′) Adapt means to change. Animals are **adapted** to live in their environment. (page 16)

amphibian (am fib′ē ən) An animal with bones that lives part of its life on land and part of its life in water. My pet frog is an **amphibian.** (page 41)

attract (ə trakt′) To pull toward. The opposite poles of two magnets will **attract** one another. (page 318)

axis (ak′sis) An imaginary line around which a planet turns. Earth spins on an **axis.** (page 370)

B

bird (bėrd) An animal with a backbone that has feathers, two legs, and wings. The **bird** flew from place to place searching for food. (page 40)

boulder (bōl′der) A large rock. The **boulder** is by the water. (page 146)

C

camouflage (kam′ə fläzh) A color or shape that makes an animal hard to see. Some animals use **camouflage** to hide themselves from danger. (page 42)

condense (kən dens′) To change from a gas to a liquid. Water vapor **condenses** on the outside of my glass of juice. (page 179)

conductor (kən duk′tər) Something that lets energy flow easily. Copper is an excellent **conductor** of electricity. (page 281)

constellation (kon′sta lā′shen) A group of stars that form a picture. I like to search the night sky for **constellations.** (page 376)

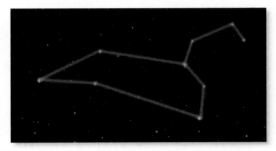

consumer (kən sü′mər) A consumer is a living thing that cannot make food. It eats food. All animals are **consumers.** (page 71)

crater (krā′tər) A hole that has the shape of a bowl. There are many **craters** on the surface of the Moon. (page 378)

D

dinosaur (dī′nə sôr) An extinct reptile that lived millions of years ago. **Dinosaurs** are large animals that lived on Earth long ago. (page 212)

E

energy (en′ər jē) The ability to do work or make change. Most plants get **energy** from the Sun. (page 271)

engine (en′jən) A machine that changes energy into force or motion. Cars, trains, and airplanes have an **engine** that helps them run. (page 400)

environment (en vī′rən mənt) All the things that surround a living thing. A cactus is a plant that grows in a desert **environment.** (page 16)

erosion (i rō′zhən) Process by which rocks and soil are moved from one place to another. Heavy rains can cause **erosion.** (page 152)

evaporate (i vap′ ə rāt) To change from a liquid to a gas. The puddles of water from the rain will **evaporate** when the Sun comes out. (page 179)

extinct (ek stingkt′) An animal or plant no longer living on Earth. Dinosaurs are now **extinct.** (page 210)

fish (fish) An animal with bones that lives in water and has gills. Many types of **fish** live in an ocean. (page 40)

flower (flou′ər) The part of a plant that makes seeds. A daisy is one kind of **flower.** (page 9)

food chain (füd chān) Plants use sunlight, air, and water to make food. Animals eat the plants. Other animals eat those animals. This is called a food chain. A coyote and a mountain lion are part of a **food chain.** (page 74)

food web (füd web) A food web is made up of the food chains in a habitat. Kelp, sea urchins, and sea otters are part of a **food web.** (page 76)

force (fôrs) A push or pull that makes something move. Jim uses **force** to move the rope. (page 304)

fossil (fos′əl) A part or a print of a plant or animal that lived long ago. Dinosaur **fossils** are in the museum. (page 207)

friction (frik′shən) A force that slows down or stops moving objects. A bicycle's brakes use **friction** to slow down. (page 312)

fuel (fyü′əl) Anything that is burned to make heat or power. We use wood as **fuel**. (page 279)

G

gas (gas) Matter that always fills the space in a container. Bubbles are filled with **gas.** (page 246)

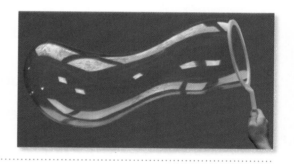

germinate (jėr′mə nāt) To begin to grow into a young plant. The seeds will soon **germinate.** (page 114)

gills (gilz) Special body parts that get oxygen from water. Fish have **gills**. (page 46)

gravity (grav′ə tē) A force that pulls things toward the center of Earth. **Gravity** will pull the leaves back to Earth. (page 306)

H

hibernate (hī′bər nāt) To spend all winter sleeping or resting. Some animals **hibernate**. (page 186)

hurricane (hėr′ə kān) A storm that starts over warm ocean waters that has hard rain and very strong winds. A **hurricane** causes heavy rain and strong winds. (page 192)

I

insect (in′sekt) An animal without bones that has three body parts and six legs. It's fun to watch **insects.** (page 52)

invent (in vent′) To make something for the first time. Alexander Graham Bell was the first to **invent** the telephone. (page 399)

L

leaves (lēvz) Parts of a plant that use sunlight, air, nutrients, and water to make food for the plant. The **leaves** on the plant are long and thin. (page 8)

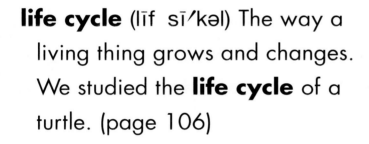

life cycle (līf sī′kəl) The way a living thing grows and changes. We studied the **life cycle** of a turtle. (page 106)

lightning (līt′ning) Lightning is a flash of electricity in the sky. We watched **lightning** flash across the sky. (page 188)

liquid (lik′wid) Matter that does not have its own shape. I like to wash my hands with **liquid** soap. (page 244)

loudness (loud′nəs) Loudness is how loud or quiet a sound is. The **loudness** of some sounds can change. (page 336)

mammal (mam′əl) An animal with bones that usually has hair or fur on its body and feeds milk to its young. Dogs, cats, and horses are some types of **mammals.** (page 40)

manufacture (man′yə fak′chər) To make by hand or machine. Many countries in the world **manufacture** clothing. (page 408)

mass (mas) How much matter an object has. I use a balance to measure **mass.** (page 239)

meteorologist (mē′tē ə rol′ə jist) A person who studies weather. The **meteorologist** predicted sunny weather. (page 407)

migrate (mī′grāt) To move from one place to another in a regular pattern. Many types of birds **migrate** in the winter. (page 184)

mineral (min′ər əl) A nonliving solid that comes from Earth. Copper is a **mineral.** (page 147)

mixture (miks′chər) Something made up of two or more things that do not change. Chicken soup is a **mixture** of liquid and solids. (page 250)

motion (mō′shen) Motion is the act of moving. A merry-go-round moves in a circular **motion.** (page 303)

natural resource (nach′ər əl rē′sôrs) Something that people use that comes from Earth. Sunlight is a **natural resource.** (page 143)

nutrients (nü′trē ənt) Materials, such as minerals, that living things need to live and grow. People get nutrients from the food they eat. (page 7)

nymph (nimf) A young insect that looks like its parent but has no wings. We found a dragonfly **nymph** in the pond by our school. (page 108)

orbit (ôr′bit) The path around something is called an orbit. Gravity keeps the Moon in its **orbit** around Earth. (page 374)

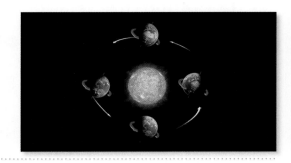

paleontologist (pā′lē on tol′ə jist) A scientist who studies fossils. **Paleontologists** study fossils to learn about life long ago. (page 207)

phase (fāz) The shape of the lighted part of the Moon is called a phase. The Moon's **phases** can be seen best at night. (page 381)

pitch (pich) Pitch is how high or low a sound is. The sound from the frog had a low **pitch.** (page 338)

pollution (pə lü′ shən) Anything harmful added to land, water, or air. Many people work hard to reduce **pollution.** (page 154)

prairie (prâr′ē) Flat land covered with grasses and having few trees. A **prairie** has a lot of grass and few trees. (page 20)

predator (pred′ə tər) A predator is an animal that hunts another animal for food. A lion is a fierce **predator.** (page 75)

prey (prā) A prey is an animal that is hunted for food. Sea stars are the **prey** of sea otters. (page 75)

producer (prə dü′sər) A producer is a living thing that makes its own food. A green plant is a **producer.** (page 71)

property (prop′ər tē) Something about an object that you can observe with your senses. An object's color is one kind of **property.** (page 240)

recycle (rē sī′kəl) To change something so that it can be used again. My family **recycles** aluminum cans. (page 156)

reflect (ri flekt′) To bounce back. A mirror can **reflect** light. (page 282)

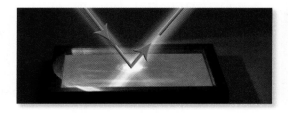

repel (ri pel′) To push away. The north ends of magnets will **repel** one another. (page 318)

reptile (rep′tīl) An animal with bones that has dry, scaly skin. Snakes are **reptiles.** (page 41)

roots (rüts) Parts of a plant that hold the plant in place and that take in water and nutrients from the soil. The **roots** of the old oak tree are deep inside the ground. (page 8)

rotation (rō tā′shən) Spinning on an axis. It takes about one year for Earth to make one **rotation** around the Sun. (page 370)

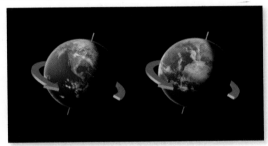

S

sand (sand) Sand is made up of tiny pieces of rock. Some plants do not grow well in **sand.** (page 146)

satellite (sat′l īt) An object that revolves around another object. Meteorologists study pictures taken by **satellites** to predict weather. (page 407)

seed coat (sēd kōt) The hard outer covering of a seed. The **seed coat** protects the seed. (page 114)

seedling (sēd′ling) A young plant. The tree **seedling** grows into a tree. (page 114)

shadow (shad′ō) A shadow is made when something blocks the light. The tree makes a **shadow.** (page 284)

simple machine (sim′pəl mə shēn) A tool with few or no moving parts that makes work easier. Workers often use **simple machines** to help them build things. (page 314)

solar energy (sō′lər en′ərjē) Solar energy uses heat and light from the Sun. My calculator runs on **solar energy.** (page 272)

solar system (sō′lər sis′tem) The Sun, the planets and their moons, and other objects that orbit the Sun. Earth is in our **solar system.** (page 382)

solid (sol′id) Matter that has its own shape and takes up space. The case that hold the supplies is a **solid.** (page 242)

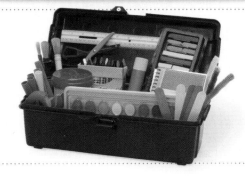

source (sôrs) A place from which something comes. A lamp is one **source** of light. (page 278)

states of matter (stāts uv mat′ər) The three states of matter are solids, liquids, and gases. Water is a liquid **state of matter.** (page 242)

stem (stem) Part of a plant that holds it up and that carries water and nutrients to the leaves. The **stem** is long and green. (page 8)

T

technology (tek nol′ə jē) How people change nature to meet their needs and wants. People use **technology** every day. (page 399)

tornado (tôr nā′ dō) Very strong wind that comes down from clouds in the shape of a funnel. A **tornado** touched down near our town. (page 190)

transportation (tran′spər tā′ shən) Ways to move people or things. Today, **transportation** makes travel easier and faster than ever before. (page 400)

V

vaccine (vak sēn′) Medicine that can prevent a disease. Mia got a shot of the flu **vaccine.** (page 402)

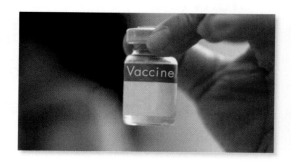

vibrate (vī′brāt) To move back and forth very fast. A flute makes the air **vibrate** to make sounds. (page 335)

water cycle (wȯ′tər sī′kəl) The movement of water from Earth to air and back to Earth. Water condenses and evaporates during the **water cycle.** (page 178)

weathering (weŦH′ər ing) The breaking apart and changing of rocks. **Weathering** causes sharp rocks to become smooth. (page 153)

work (wėrk) When force moves an object. It took a lot of **work** to push the sled up the hill. (page 308)

Index

This Index lists the pages on which topics appear in this book.
Page numbers after a *p* refer to a photograph. Page numbers
after a *c* refer to a chart or graph.

 A

Activities

    directed inquiry, explore. *See* Directed Inquiry, Explore

    guided inquiry, investigate. *See* Guided Inquiry, Investigate

    take-home. *See* Take-home Activities

Adapt, adaptation, 3, 16–17, 19, 21, 23, 24–25

Air, as natural resource, 144–145

Alike and different, 37, 41, 45, 117, 120–121, 131, 140–141, 218, 365, 369, 389

Amphibians, *p*35, 41, 50–51

Animal scientists, 352

Animals

    functions, of body parts, 316–317

    grouping, 58–59, 131

    growth and change, 102–112

    interdependence, 88–89

    needs of, 71–73, 274–276

    and plants, 84–86

    protecting, 158–159

    sounds of, 342–343

Antarctica, 62–63

Ants, 84

Art in science, 14, 43, 75, 117, 131, 157, 182, 188, 251, 283, 341, 379

Astronauts, 262–263

Astronomers, 392

Atmospheric scientists, 200

Attract, attraction, *p*299, 318, 320–321

Axis, *p*362, 370

 B

Backbones

    animals with, 39–51

    animals without, 52–55

Bar graph, 348–349

Biographies

    Hendrickson, Susan, 224

    Jenkins, Luther, 328

    Mota, Mario, 128

    Purgue, Alejandro, 352

    Wright, Shonte, 416

Birds, *p*34, 40, 44–45

Bones, 38–39. *See also* Backbones

Boulders, *p*138, 146

Build background, 2–3, 34–35, 66–67, 98, 100, 138–139, 170–171, 202–203, 234–235, 266–267, 298–299, 330, 362–363, 394–395

 C

Cactus, 13, 23, 116

Camouflage, *p*35, 42, 44, 52

Careers

    astronomer, 392

    atmospheric scientist, 200

    camera operator, 296

farmer, 96

forester, 168

marine biologist, 128

material scientist, 264

paleontologist, 207

plant scientist, 32

wildlife rehabilitator, 64

Cause and effect, 69, 72–73, 82, 95

Chameleon, 48

Chapter reviews. *See* Reviews, chapter

Chase, Mary Agnes, 32

Chipmunks, *p*42, 43

Clay soil, 148, 149

Communicating, 56, 131, 204, 223, 300, 327, 389, 397

Communication, and technology, 404–405

Condense, condensation, *p*170, 179

Conductor, *p*267, 281

Conservation, 154–159

Constellations, *p*362, 376, 376–377, 384–385

Consumers, 66, 71

Crater, *p*363, 378, 379

Data

collecting, 100, 122, 194, 199, 229

interpreting, 194, 195, 322, 323

recording, 122–123, 229

Day and night, 370–371

Deer, 42, 58

Desert, 22–23

Dinosaurs, *p*202, 212–217, 223

Directed inquiry, explore, 4, 26, 68, 100, 140, 172, 204, 236, 268, 300, 332, 365

Diving beetle, 58

Dragonfly, 108–109

Drawing conclusions, 173, 179, 184, 192, 199, 237, 247, 249, 261

Drought, 177

Earth, 152, *p*382, 386

Effect, and cause. *See* Cause and effect

Electricity, 288–289

Energy, *p*266, 271, 274–276

Engine, 400

Engineers, 328

Environment, of plants, 3, 16

Erosion, *p*138, 152, 153

Estimating and measuring, 17, 89-90, 92–93, 95, 124–125, 147, 217, 220-221, 243, 258–259, 292-293, 300, 311, 324–325

Evaporate, evaporation, *p*170, 179, 232, 251, 254–255

Experiment. *See* Full Inquiry, Experiment

Experimenting. *See* Directed Inquiry, Explore; Full Inquiry, Experiment; Guided Inquiry, Investigate

Explore. *See* Directed Inquiry, Explore

Extinct, *p*203, 210

Fall season, 184–185

FEMA (Federal Emergency Management Agency) website, 159

Ferns, 14, 15

Fish, *p*34, 40, 46–47

Florida, 85

Flowers, 2, 9, 12, 13, 117

Flying squirrels, 42, 43

Food

as energy, 276–277

in space, 262–263

Food chains, 67, 78–79

Food webs, 67, 74–83, 76–83

changing, 82–83

ocean, 80–81

Force, p299, 304–305

Foresters, 168

Fossils, p202, 207–211, 218–220, 223

Freezing, 252, 253

Friction, p298, 312

Frogs, p41, 50–51, 58

Fruit, 12

Fuel, p266, 279

Full inquiry, experiment, 228–229, 232

Gaffer, 296

Gases, 246–247, 253, 254–255, 340–341

Geography, 85, 181, 183, 185, 187

Germinate, 99, 114

Gills, p34, 46

Giraffes, 71

Graphing, 59, 100, 221, 348–349

Grassland, 74–76

Gravity, p298, 306–307

Growth and change

animals, 102–113

human beings, 118–121

insects, 108–109, 122–123

plants, 114–117

Guided inquiry, investigate, 26–27, 90–91, 122–123, 194–195, 218–219, 256–257, 290–291, 322–323, 346, 384–385, 410–411

Habitats, 16–25, 72–73

Health in science, 13, 155, 276, 402–403

Heat, 278–279, 280–281

Heating matter, 254–255

Hendrickson, Susan, 224

Heredity, 112–113, 120–121

Hibernate, hibernation, 43, p171, 186

Horses, 110–111

How to Read Science

alike and different, 37, 365

cause and effect, 69

drawing conclusions, 173, 237

important details, 333

infer, 101, 269

picture clues, 141

predict, 5

put things in order, 301

retell, 205, 397

Hubble **space telescope,** 392

Human beings

growth and change, 118–121

needs of, 276–277

Hummingbirds, 44

Humus, 148–149

Hurricanes, p171, 192–193

Hypothesizing, 228–229

Iguanas, 49

Important details, 333, 338, 343, 351

Inclined plane, p315

Inferring, 27, 31, 68, 91, 100, 109, 122–123, 127, 172, 173, 236, 237, 268, 274, 289, 290, 295, 415

Insects, p35, 52–53, 55, 84

    life cycles, 108–109, 122–123

Internet, using, 159, 177, 387

Invent, p394, 399

Investigate, See Guided Inquiry, Investigate

Jenkins, Luther, 328

Krill, 63

Leaves, 3, 8, 14, 28, 29

Lever, 316

Life cycle, 98, 104–111

    dragonfly, 108–109

    horse, 110–111

    turtle, 104–107

Light, 282–283

Lighting operator, 296

Lightning, p171, 188

Liquids, 234, 244–245, 253, 254–255, 340–341

Lizards, p41

Loudness, p330, 336–337

Magnets, 318–321, 322–323

Mammals, p34, 38, 40, 42–43

Manufacture, p395, 408–409

Maps, 181, 183, 185, 187

Marine biologists, 128

Mars, 390–391

Marsh, 24–25, 386

Mass, 234, 239

Material scientists, 264

Math in science

    estimating and measuring. See Estimating and measuring

    graphing and charting, 162–163, 196–197, 220–221, 258–259, 292–293, 412

    bar graph, 349

    grouping and sorting, 58–59, 241

    number sentences, 55, 162, 405

    patterns, 17, 28–29, 285, 381

    temperature, measuring, 232, 253, 256–257

Matter, 239–261

    changing, 248–255

    properties of, 240–241

    states of, 242–248, 353

Maze, building, 410–411

Measuring and estimating. See Estimating and measuring

Melting, 254–255

Mercury, p382, 386

Meteorologist, p395, 407

Migrate, migration, p171, 184

Minerals, p138, 147

Mixture, 235, 250–251

Models, making and using, 36, 90–91, 123, 218–219, 365, 384

Moon, the, 378–381

Mosses, 14, 15

Mota, Mario, 128

Motion, p298, 303, p313

and force, 310–311

and gravity, 324–325

NASA (National Aeronautics and Space Administration), 262–263

careers at, 128, 200, 264, 328, 416

mission to Mars, 390–391

satellites, 63, 166–167, p394, 407

studies penguins, 62–63

Natural resources, 138–139, 143, 154–159

Neptune, p383

Nests, building, 86–87

Night and day, 370–371

NOAA (National Oceanic and Atmospheric Administration) website, 177

Nutrients, 2, 7

Nymph, 98, 108

Observing, 140, 141, 219, 256, 261, 290, 295, 323, 332, 333, 351, 385, 410

Octopus, 54, 56, 58

Oil spill, 82–83

Operational definitions, making, 384

Opportunity (space rover), 391

Orbit, p363, 374, 386, 386–387

Paleontologists, p203, 207, 224

Patterns, 17, 28–29

Penguins, 45, 58, 62–63

Performance assessments, 355, 419

Peticolas, Laura, 392

Phase, p363, 381

Picture clues, 141, 149, 150–151, 165

Pinecones, 14

Pitch, p331, 338–339

Plants

and animals, 84–86

classifying, 12–15

environment, 15–17

life cycles, 114–117

as living things, 103

as natural resource, 150–151

needs of, 4, 7, 26–27, 71–73, 145, 274–276

parts of, 2–3, 7–9

protecting, 158–159

woodland, 16–19

Pluto, p383

Poems

Apple Shadows, 358–359

Little Seeds, 134–135

The Spring Wind, 230–231

This Happy Day, 422–423

Pollution, p139, 154–155, 401

Prairie habitat, 3, 19–21

Predators, 66, 75

Predicting, 4, 5, 10, 31, 256, 257, 322–323, 346–347, 410

Prey, 66, 75

Producers, 66, 71

Properties, of matter, 234, 240–241

Pulley, p315

Put things in order, 301, 307, 312, 327

Rainfall, 172

Recycling, p139, 157, 162–163

Reflect, reflection, p267, 283

Repel, p299, 318

Reptiles, p35, 41, 48–49

Retelling, 205, 209, 211, 223, 397, 403, 409, 415

Reviews, chapter, 30–31, 60–61, 94–95, 126–127, 164–165, 198–199, 222–223, 260–261, 294–295, 326, 350, 388, 414

Reviews, unit, 130–131, 225–226, 353–354, 417–418

Rocks, 146–148

Roots, 2, 8, 14

Rotation, of planets, p362, 370

Sand, p138, 146, 148, 149

Satellites, space, 63, 166–167, p394, 407

Saturn, p383

Scaffolded inquiry

directed inquiry, explore. *See* Directed Inquiry, Explore

full inquiry, experiment. *See* Full Inquiry, Experiment

guided inquiry, investigate. *See* Guided Inquiry, Investigate

Science Fair Projects, 136, 232, 360, 424

Science process skills

classify, 194, 195

collecting data, 100, 122, 194, 199, 229

controlling variables, 132

communicating, 56, 131, 204, 223, 300, 327, 389, 397

estimating and measuring, 89, 90, 220, 300

inferring, 31, 68, 91, 100, 109, 123, 127, 131, 172, 236, 237, 268, 274, 289, 290, 415

interpreting data, 194, 323

investigating. *See* Guided inquiry, investigate

making and using models, 36, 90–91, 123, 218, 218–219, 365, 384

making definitions, 384

making hypotheses, 228–229

observing, 140, 141, 165, 219, 256, 261, 290, 295, 323, 332, 333, 351, 385, 410

predicting, 4, 5, 10, 31, 322–323, 346–347, 410

Scientific methods, using, 232

Sea otter, 79

Seasons, 180–187, 196–197, 199, 374–375

Seed coat, 98, 114

Seedlings, 99, 114

Seeds, 9, 10–11, 14, 114

Shadows, p267, 284–285, 292–293

Shelter, 86–87

Simple machines, p298, 314–315

Skunks, 38, 39

Sky, 376–379

Snakes, 36, 37, 48, 49, 59

Social studies in science, 18, 20, 85, 279, 286, 314, 374

Soil, 140, 148–149, 228–229

Solar energy, p266, 272–273

Solar system, p362, 382–387, p383

Solids, 235, 242–243, 252, 253, 340–341

Songs

"Go Find a Fossil," 206

"Good Partners," 70

"Hi, Little Turtle," 102

"Listen to the Sounds," 334

"Natural Resources," 142

"Plants," 6

"Technology Helps Us All," 398

"The Sun," 366

"They're All Matter!," 238

"Use Some Force!," 302

"What Has Backbones?," 38

"What's the Weather?," 174

"Where Do We Get Energy?," 220

Sound, 340–343

Source, p266, 278

Space food, 262–263

Space rovers, 390–391, 416

Spiders, 55

Spirit (space rover), 390

Spring season, 180–181

Stars, 376–377

Stems, 2, 9, 14

Summer, 182–183

Sun, the, 367–369, 372–373, p382

Take-home activities, 29, 32, 59, 63, 64, 93, 96, 124–125, 128, 163, 167, 197, 200, 221, 224, 263, 293, 296, 349, 352, 387, 392, 413

Target Reading Skills

alike and different, 37, 41, 45, 117, 120–121, 131, 140, 218, 369, 389

cause and effect, 69, 72–73

drawing conclusions, 173, 179, 184, 192, 199, 237

important details, 333, 338, 343, 351, 365

inferring, 27, 31, 68, 91, 100, 109, 122–123, 127, 172, 173, 236, 237, 268, 274, 289, 295

picture clues, 141, 149, 150–151, 165

predicting, 322–323

put things in order, 301, 307, 312, 327

retelling, 205, 209, 211, 223, 397, 403, 409, 415

Technology, p394, 399

Technology in science, 53, 159, 177, 317, 376

Temperature, measuring, 232, 256–257

Test Talk, 129, 225–226, 353, 417

Thunderstorm, 189

Time, measuring, 124–125

Toads, 51

Tornadoes, p170, 190–191

Transportation, p395, 400–401

Trees, 12, 15, 16–17

Turtles, 41, p64, p98, 102–107

life cycle, 104–107

Unit reviews. See Reviews, unit

Uranus, p383

V

Vaccine, *p*394, 402

Vapor, *p*170, 179, 252

Venus, *p*382, 386

Vibrate, vibration, *p*330, 335

Vocabulary, 3, 35, 60, 67, 99, 139, 171, 203, 267, 299, 331, 395

W

Water, as natural resource, 144–145

Water cycle, *p*170, 178–179

Water vapor, *p*170, 179, 252

Weather, 175–178, 188–197, 199

Weathering, *p*138, 153

Wedge, 316, 317

Wheel and axle, *p*315

Wildlife rehabilitator, 64

Windy day, 175

Winter, 186–187

Woodland habitat, 16–18

Work, *p*298, 308–309

Worms, 36, 37

Wright, Shonte, 416

Writing in science, 9, 49, 51, 87, 95, 111, 113, 127, 144, 153, 165, 180, 186, 190, 199, 213, 215, 223, 245, 247, 255, 261, 272, 281, 295, 305, 309, 321, 327, 337, 344, 351, 371, 373, 389, 401, 407, 415

y

Yeast, 68, 69

Credits

Text

"Little Seeds" from *The Winds that Come From Far Away and Other Poems* by Else Holmelund Minarik. Copyright ©1964 by Else Holmelund Minarik. Used by permission of HarperCollins Publishers.

"The Spring Wind" from *River Winding: Poems* by Charolotte Zolotow; Copyright ©1970 by Charlotte Zolotow. Reprinted by permission of Sott Treimel, NY.

"This Happy Day" from *The Little Hill* by Harry Behn (Harcourt Brace, 1949).

"Apple Shadows" reprinted from *Black Earth, Gold Sun* by Patricia Hubbell with permission of Marshall Cavendish. Copyright ©2001 by Cavendish Children's Books.

Illustrations

29, 301, 327, 362, 367–368, 370–374, 376, 378, 380, 382, 388 Bob Kayganich; 69 Patrick Gnan; 201–203, 205-208 Big Sesh Studios; 344 Philip Williams; 365 Mary Teichman.

Photographs

Every effort has been made to secure permission and provide appropriate credit for photographic material. The publisher deeply regrets any omission and pledges to correct errors called to its attention in subsequent editions.

Unless otherwise acknowledged, all photographs are the property of Scott Foresman, a division of Pearson Education.

Photo locators denoted as follows: Top (T), Center (C), Bottom (B), Left (L), Right (R), Background (Bkgd).

Cover: (C) ©Chase Swift/Corbis, (B) ©Walter Hodges/Corbis, (Bkgd) ©Ralph A. Clevenger/Corbis, (Bkgd) ©George Grall/NGS Image Collection

Title Page: ©Tom Brakefield/Corbis

Front Matter: ii ©DK Images; iii (TR, BR) ©DK Images; v ©DK Images; vi (CL) ©David Middleton/NHPA Limited, (CL) ©Stephen Dalton/NHPA Limited; vii (CR) Tom Brakefield/Corbis, (B) Geoff Moon/ Frank Lane Picture Agency/Corbis; viii (CL) Nigel J. Dennis/NHPA Limited, (B) William Bernard/Corbis; ix Andy Rouse/ NHPA Limited; x (CL) ©Stone/Getty Images, (CL) ©Steve Terrill/Corbis, (B) ©DK Images; xi ©DK Images; xiii ©DK Images; xiv ©Charles Gupton/ Corbis; xv ©Kelly-Mooney Photography/Corbis; xvi (CL) ©Lester Lefkowitz/Corbis, (CL) Getty Images; xvii (CR) ©John Gillmoure/Corbis, (Bkgd) ©Handout/Reuters/ Corbis; xviii (CL, B) NASA Image Exchange, (CL) Getty Images, (BC) ©NASA/JPL/ Handout/Reuters/Corbis; xix ©Reuters/Corbis; xxiv NASA; xxv Getty Images; xxix ©Royalty-Free/Corbis; xxxi ©Ed Bock/Corbis.

Unit A: Divider: (Bkgd) Digital Vision, (CC) Digital Vision; **Chapter 1:** 1 (C) ©David Middleton/NHPA Limited, (BR) ©Stephen Dalton/NHPA Limited, (TR) Brand X Pictures; 2 (BR) ©DK Images, (T) Corbis; 3 (BL) ©DK Images, (BR) Richard Hamilton Smith/Corbis, (Bkgd) Corbis, (TR) ©Stephen Dalton/NHPA Limited, (CL) ©Eric Crichton/Corbis; 6 (C) Corbis, (TR) ©Stephen Dalton/NHPA Limited; 7 (BR) Brand X Pictures, (TR) Hemera Technologies; 8 (TL, BL, BC) ©DK Images; 10 Brand X Pictures; 11 (CL) ©Ted Mead/PhotoLibrary, (TR, BR) ©DK Images, (TL) ©Michael Boys/Corbis, (CR) ©ChromaZone Images/Index Stock Imagery, (BL) ©Scott Camazine/Photo Researchers, Inc.; 12 (TL) Peter Anderson/©DK Images, (CR) ©Cosmo Condina/Getty Images; 13 (CL) Steve Kaufman/Corbis, (CR) Ted Levin/ Animals Animals/Earth Scenes; 14 Getty Images; 15 (TR, CR) ©DK Images, (TL) ©Bill Ross/Corbis, (CL) ©Ed Reschke/Peter Arnold, Inc., (BL) ©Ted Mead/ PhotoLibrary, (BR) Getty Images; 16 (CR) ©M.P. Kahl/DRK Photo, (TL) ©DK Images; 17 (CL)©Royalty-Free/Corbis, (TR) ©DK Images; 18 (TL) ©Medford Taylor/NGS Image Collection, (BR) ©Eric Crichton/Corbis; 19 (TR, BR) ©DK Images, (C) ©Bob Wickham/PhotoLibrary; 20 (T) ©Pat O'Hara/Corbis, (BR) Neil Fletcher and Matthew Ward/©DK Images; 21 (T) Getty Images, (TR) ©Pat O'Hara/Corbis, (BR) ©David Muench/Corbis; 22 (BR) ©Ronald Martin, (TL) Getty Images; 23 (C) Randall Hyman Photography, (BR) ©Patti Murray/Animals/Earth Scenes, (TR) ©Steve Kaufman/Corbis; 24 (TL, BR) Brand X Pictures; 25 (TR) Image Quest 3-D/NHPA Limited, (BR) ©OSF/Animals Animals/Earth Scenes, ©David Muench/

Corbis; 26 ©George D. Lepp/Corbis; 28 (CL, BL) Matthew Ward/©DK Images, (T) Hemera Technologies; 29 ©Klein/Hubert/Peter Arnold, Inc.; 30 (BR) ©Pat O'Hara/ Corbis, (TR) ©Richard Hamilton Smith/Corbis, (TL, CL, CC, CR) ©DK Images; 31 (TR) ©DK Images, (CL) ©Roy Rainford/Robert Harding Picture Library, Ltd.; 32 (BL) Getty Images, (TL, CL) Hunt Institute for Botanical Documentation/Carnegie Mellon University, Pittsburgh, PA; **Chapter 2:** 33 (C) Tom Brakefield/Corbis, (CR) Brand X Pictures; 34 (BL) ©Don Enger/Animals Animals/Earth Scenes, (BR) Getty Images; 35 (CR) ©Tom Brakefield/Corbis, (TR) ©Joe McDonald/Corbis, (BR) ©Buddy Mays/Corbis, (BL) ©Jean-Louis Le Moigne/NHPA Limited; 37 (Bkgd) ©Alan G. Nelson/Animals Animals/Earth Scenes, (TR) Brand X Pictures, (CL) ©Breck P. Kent/Animals Animals/ Earth Scenes, (BCL) ©Joe McDonald/Animals Animals/Earth Scenes; 38 ©Alan G. Nelson/Animals Animals/Earth Scenes; 39 (BR) ©W. Perry Conway/Corbis, (TL) ©DK Images; 40 (BL) ©Joe McDonald/Corbis, (BC) ©George D.Lepp/Corbis, (BR) Getty Images, (TL) Hemera Technologies; 41 (BL) Getty Images, (BR) ©Tom Brakefield/Corbis; 42 (BL) ©Royalty-Free/Corbis, (TR) ©Joe McDonald/Corbis, (TL) Getty Images, ©D. Robert & Lorri Franz/Corbis; 43 ©Breck P. Kent/Animals Animals/Earth Scenes; 44 (TR) ©Jean-Louis Le Moigne/NHPA Limited, (B) ©Kent Wood/Photo Researchers, Inc., (TL) ©DK Images; 45 ©DK Images; 46 (CR, BL) ©DK Images, (TL) ©Comstock; 47 (TR, CR) ©DK Images; 48 (C) ©Stephen Dalton/ NHPA Limited, (BL) ©Daniel Heuclin/NHPA Limited, (TL) Hemera Technologies; 49 ©Zig Leszczynski/Animals Animals/Earth Scenes; 50 (B) ©Carmela Leszczynski/ Animals Animals/Earth Scenes, (TL) Hemera Technologies; 51 (CL) Getty Images, (C) ©Kim Taylor/Bruce Coleman Collection; 52 (TL, C) ©DK Images, (B) ©Geoff Moon/Frank Lane Picture Agency/Corbis; 53 ©OSF/D. Clyne/Animals Animals/ Earth Scenes; 54 (TL, C) ©DK Images; 55 (CR) ©Niall Benvie/Corbis, (TR, CR)©DK Images; 56 ©Dale Sanders/Masterfile Corporation; 58 (C, BC, BR) ©DK Images, (BL) ©Royalty-Free/Corbis, (CL) ©Carmela Leszczynski/Animals Animals/Earth Scenes; 59 (BL) ©DK Images, (B) ©Daniel Heuclin/NHPA Limited; 60 (TR, CL, BR) Getty Images, (TL) ©Tom Brakefield/Corbis, (TCL) ©DK Images, (TCR) ©Joe McDonald/Corbis, (CR) ©Don Enger/Animals Animals/Earth Scenes; 61 (TR) ©DK Images, (CL, CR) Hemera Technologies; 62 (Bkgd) Map Resources, (C) ©Marian Bacon/Animals Animals/Earth Scenes, (B) Getty Images; 63 (TR) ©Andrew Syred/ Photo Researchers, Inc., (T)©Royalty-Free/Corbis, (BR) MFSC/NASA, (C) ©Orbital Sciences Corporation/Photo Researchers, Inc.; 64 (BL) ©Niall Benvie/Corbis, (CL)©George Grall/National Geographic/Getty Images, (TR) ©Raymond Gehman/NGS Image Collection; **Chapter 3:** 65 (TC) ©Nigel J. Dennis/NHPA Limited, (TR) Getty Images; 66 (TC) ©Clem Haagner/Gallo Images/Corbis, (B) ©Kennan Ward/Corbis; 67 (BR) ©Randy Morse/Animals Animals/Earth Scenes, (CR) ©Stephen Frink/Corbis, (BR) ©James Watt/Animals Animals/Earth Scenes, (CR) ©Steve Bein/Corbis, (CR) ©Andrew J. Martinez/Photo Researchers, Inc., (TR) ©Sanford/Agliolo/Corbis, (TR) ©Amos Nachoum/Corbis; 69 (Bkgd) ©Clem Haagner/Gallo Images/Corbis, (TR) Getty Images; 70 Clem Haagner/Gallo Images/Corbis; 71 (R) ©Peter Johnson/Corbis, (TR) Hemera Technologies; 72 (TL) Getty Images, (B) ©Clem Haagner/Gallo Images/Corbis; 73 ©Ian Beames/ Ecoscene/Corbis; 74 (BL) ©Royalty-Free/Corbis, (BR) ©Joe McDonald/Corbis, (TL) Frank Greenaway/©DK Images; 75 (BR) ©William Bernard/Corbis, (B) ©Gaoil Shumway/Getty Images, (CR) ©Royalty-Free/Corbis; 76 (TR) ©DK Images, (TL, CR) ©Joe McDonald/Corbis, (BR) ©Stephen Krasemann/NHPA Limited, (CL)©Royalty-Free/Corbis; 77 (CL) ©Gaoil Shumway/Getty Images, (TC) ©Jim Zipp/Photo Researchers, Inc.; 78 (CL) ©Randy Morse/Animals Animals/Earth Scenes, (BC) ©Stephen Frink/Corbis, (CR) ©Andrew J. Martinez/Photo Researchers, Inc., (TL) Brand X Pictures; 79 ©Kennan Ward/Corbis; 80 (TC) ©James Watt/Animals Animals/Earth Scenes, (BR) ©Andrew J. Martinez/Photo Researchers, Inc., (CR) ©Stephen Frink/Corbis, (CL) ©Randy Morse/Animals Animals/Earth Scenes, (TL) ©Andrew J. Martinez/Photo Researchers, Inc.; 81 (T) ©Amos Nachoum/Corbis, (CR) ©Sanford/Agliolo/Corbis, (BC) ©Steve Bein/Corbis; 82 (T) ©Sanford/ Agliolo/Corbis, (BL) ©Bettmann/Corbis; 83 ©Sanford/Agliolo/Corbis; 84 (B) ©Michael and Patricia Fogden/Corbis, (TL) ©DK Images; 85 ©Fred McConnaughey/Photo Researchers, Inc.; 86 (BL) ©Darrell Gulin/Corbis, (TL) Getty Images, (BR) ©Farrell Grehan/Corbis; 87 ©DK Images; 88 (CL) ©Pete Atkinson/ NHPA Limited, (TL) NHPA Limited; 89 (CC) ©Eric and David Hosking/Corbis, (TC) ©Rob C. Nunnington/Gallo Images/Corbis, (TR) ©Richard Murphy; 90 ©Kennan Ward/Corbis; 92 (TR) ©Joe McDonald/Corbis, (BR) ©D. Robert and Lorri Franz/ Corbis, (Bkgd) ©William Manning/Corbis, (BL) Getty Images, (CL) Jane Burton/©DK Images; 94 (BR) ©Clem Haagner/Gallo Images/Corbis, (TC) ©Stephen Krasemann/NHPA Limited, (TR) ©Randy Morse/ Animals Animals/Earth Scenes, (CL, CR) ©Royalty-Free/Corbis, (C) ©Joe McDonald/Corbis; 95 (CL) ©George H. H. Huey/Corbis, (CR) ©Norbert Rosing/ NGS Image Collection, (TR) ©Andrew J. Martinez/Photo Researchers, Inc.; 96 (T,

L) Getty Images, (B, BL) Brand X Pictures, (TL) ©The Image Bank/Getty Images;
Chapter 4: 97 (C) ©Andy Rouse/NHPA Limited, (CR) ©Paul A. Sounders/Corbis;
98 (TL) ©Jonathan Blair/Corbis, (BL) ©Robert Thompson/NHPA Limited, (CL)
©Soames Summerhays/Photo Researchers, Inc., (C) ©Royalty-Free/Corbis, (BR)
©DK Images; 99 (BR) ©Carol Cohen/Corbis, (Bkgd) ©Tom Brakefield/Corbis, (TL)
©DK Images; 101 (TR) ©Paul A. Sounders/Corbis, (CL) ©Royalty-Free/Corbis, (CR)
©David Young Wolff/PhotoEdit; 102 ©Tom Brakefield/Corbis; 103 Getty Images;
104 (TL) Getty Images, (CR) ©Peter Johnson/Corbis, (CL) ©Jonathan Blair/Corbis;
105 ©C. Allan Morgan/Peter Arnold, Inc.; 106 (CL) ©Jonathan Blair/Corbis, (BL)
©Soames Summerhays/Photo Researchers, Inc.; 106 Getty Images; 107 ©DK
Images; 108 (CC) ©DK Images, (TL) Courtesy of Digital Dragonflies, (BL) ©Robert
Thompson/NHPA Limited; 109 ©DK Images; 110 (CL, CR) ©DK Images, (TL) Getty
Images; 111 Bob Langrish/©DK Images; 112 (BL) ©Julie Habel/Corbis, (TR) ©Tim
Davis/Corbis, (TL) ©DK Images; 113 ©Kevin Schafer/NHPA Limited; 114 (BL, BC,
BR) ©DK Images, (TL) Brand X Pictures; 115 ©DK Images; 116 (TL) Brand X
Pictures, (R) ©Robert Landau/Corbis, (BC) Getty Images; 117 ©DK Images; 118
(TL, BR) ©DK Images; 119 (CC, CR, BL, BC) ©DK Images; 120 (TL, C, BL, BC) ©DK
Images; 121 ©DK Images; 122 (TR) ©Gladden William Willis/Animals Animals/
Earth Scenes, (TC, TR) ©T. Kitchin & V. Hurst/NHPA Limited, (TR) ©Stephen Dalton/
NHPA Limited; 124 (C) ©Albert Normandin/Masterfile Corporation, (B) ©DK
Images, (CC) Getty Images, (C) ©Michael Newman/PhotoEdit, (CL) ©Robert
Pickett/Corbis, (BL) ©Richard Shiell/Animals Animals/Earth Scenes, (BR) ©Kevin
Schafer/Corbis; 125 (BL) ©DK Images, (CL) ©Stephen Dalton/NHPA Limited, (BL)
©George Bernard/NHPA Limited, (CC) Getty Images; 126 (TR, CL, CR, BL, BR)
©DK Images, (CR) ©Gary W. Carter/Corbis, (CR) ©Jonathan Blair/Corbis, (CR)
©Soames Summerhays/Photo Researchers, Inc., (TC) ©Robert Thompson/NHPA
Limited, (CC) ©Carol Cohen/Corbis; 127 ©DK Images; 128 (B) ©Fred Bruemmer/
DRK Photo, (TC) ©Carl & Ann Purcell/Corbis, (CL) NASA, (C) ©Stone/Getty
Images; 130 (BL) ©Tom Brakefield/Corbis, (TCL) ©Alan G. Nelson/Animals
Animals/Earth Scenes, (TL) Corbis, (CL) ©Clem Haagner/Gallo Images/Corbis;
131 (TR) ©Andrew J. Martinez/Photo Researchers, Inc., (CR) ©Eric and David
Hosking/Corbis, (CR) ©Don Enger/Animals Animals/Earth Scenes; 132 (TR) ©Theo
Allofs/Corbis, (TR) ©Lynda Richardson/Corbis; 134 (Bkgd) ©Michael Boys/Corbis,
(TL) ©Tim Wright/Corbis; 135 ©Bohemian Nomad Picturemakers/Corbis; 136 (BC)
©Image Quest 3-D/NHPA Limited, (C) ©Michael & Patricia Fogden/Corbis,
(Bkgd) ©Stone/Getty Images, (TC) Getty Images.

Unit B: Divider: ©Gavin Hellier/Getty Images; **Chapter 5:** 137 (TC) ©Stone/
Getty Images, (C) ©Steve Terrill/Corbis; 138 (BR) Grant Heilman Photography,
(BL) ©DK Images; 139 (CR) ©Royalty-Free/Corbis, (BR) ©Pete Soloutos/Corbis;
141 (TR) ©Stone/Getty Images, (C) ©David M. Dennis/Animals Animals/Earth
Scenes; 143 ©DK Images; 144 Getty Images; 145 (TL) ©Roy Morsch/Corbis, (BL)
©DK Images, (BR) ©Craig Tuttle/Corbis, (TR) Getty Images; 146 (B) ©Royalty-
Free/Corbis, Hemera Technologies; 147 (TR, CL) ©DK Images, (BR) Brand X
Pictures, (CL) ©Mark A. Schneider/Visuals Unlimited; 148 ©DK Images; 149 ©DK
Images; 150 (CR) ©Donna Disario/Corbis, (CL, BR) Getty Images, (CR) ©Rob
Blakers/Photo Library; 151 (CR, BR) ©Royalty-Free/Corbis, (TL, CL) Getty Images,
(BL) Corbis; 152 (CR) ©Royalty-Free/Corbis, (B) Grant Heilman Photography, (TL)
Hemera Technologies; 153 (CR) ©Joe McDonald/Animals Animals/Earth Scenes,
(B) ©Lester Lefkowitz/Corbis; 154 (T) Digital Vision, (TL) ©ThinkStock/SuperStock,
(T) ©Gary Meszaros/Visuals Unlimited, (BR) ©Charles E. Rotker/Corbis; 156 (TL)
©Corbis, (BC) ©Pete Soloutos/Corbis, (BL) ©Ryan McVay/Getty Images; 157
©Eric Fowke/PhotoEdit; 158 (CL) ©Phil Schermeister/Corbis, (TL) Getty Images,
(R) ©Steve Terrill/Corbis; 159 ©Momatiuk Eastcott/Animals Animals/Earth Scenes;
160 ©Robert Pickett/Corbis; 162 ©Susan Steinkamp/Corbis; 164 (TC) ©Mark
A. Schneider/Visuals Unlimited, (B) ©Lester Lefkowitz/Corbis, (CR) ©Charles E.
Rotker/Corbis, (CL) ©Owaki-Kulla/Corbis, (TL) ©Pete Soloutos/Corbis, (CC) Grant
Heilman Photography; 165 (CL) ©Stone/Getty Images, (CR) Getty Images; 166
(BR) Corbis, (Bkgd) ©Royalty-Free/Corbis, (TR) Getty Images, (BL) ©Reuters/Corbis;
167 (TL, C) Getty Images; 168 (T) Getty Images, (TL) ©Lynda Richardson/Corbis,
(CL) ©Jonathan Blair/Corbis, (BL) ©Macduff Everton/Corbis, (B) ©Royalty-Free/
Corbis, (R) Tim Ridley/©DK Images; **Chapter 6:** 169 (C) ©Jim Zuckerman/Corbis,
(TC) Getty Images; 170 (B) ©Sam Abell/NGS Image Collection, (B) ©Alan. R.
Moller/Getty Images; 171 (BR) ©Joseph H. Bailey/NGS Image Collection, (BR)
©George McCarthy/Corbis, (TR) ©Annie Griffiths Belt/NGS Image Collection,
(CR) ©A & J Verkaik/Corbis; 173 ©Alan. R. Moller/Getty Images; 174 (C) ©Otto
Rogge/Corbis, (Bkgd) ©Bill Ross/Corbis; 175 (TR) ©Corbis, (B) ©DK Images;
176 (CL) ©Gene E. Moore, (TR) ©Phil Schermeister/NGS Image Collection, (TL)
©Stone/Getty Images; 177 (TR) Tom L. McKnight, (CR) ©Richard Hamilton Smith/
Corbis; 178 (CC) ©Sam Abell/NGS Image Collection, (TL) Hemera Technologies;

180 (BR) Getty Images, (TL) Hemera Technologies, (BR) ©Tom Brakefield/Corbis;
181 (CL, BL) Getty Images, (TL) ©Dennis MacDonald/PhotoEdit; 182 (TL) Hemera
Technologies, (B) ©John Conrad/Corbis; 183 (TL) ©James Schwabel/Panoramic
Images, Chicago, (BL) ©D. Robert and Lorri Franz/Corbis, (CL) ©Michael
Boys/Corbis; 184 (TL) Hemera Technologies, (BR) ©Gary W. Carter/Corbis;
185 (CL) ©Stone/Getty Images, (B) ©Lowell Georgia/Corbis; 186 (TL) Hemera
Technologies, (BR) ©Marty Stoufer/Animals Animals/Earth Scenes; 187 (BL)
©Comstock Images/Getty Images, (TL, CL) Getty Images; 188 ©DK Images; 189
(CL) ©A & J Verkaik/Corbis, (TR) Getty Images; 190 (TL) ©Steve Bronstein/Getty
Images, (TL) Hemera Technologies; 191 ©Alan. R. Moller/Getty Images; 192
Hemera Technologies; 193 (CL) ©Annie Griffiths Belt/NGS Image Collection, (CL)
Getty Images; 194 Corbis, 196 (Bkgd) ©Gabe Palmer/Corbis, (BC) ©Stone/Getty
Images; 197 (CL, CR) Hemera Technologies, (TL) Getty Images; 198 (TC) ©A & J
Verkaik/Corbis, (TR) ©Marty Stoufer/Animals Animals/Earth Scenes, (CC) ©Annie
Griffiths Belt/NGS Image Collection, (CR) ©Stone/Getty Images, (BC) ©Alan. R.
Moller/Getty Images, (BR) ©D. Robert and Lorri Franz/Corbis; 199 (CL) ©Ariel
Skelley/Corbis, (TR) ©Dennis MacDonald/PhotoEdit; 200 (BR) ©SYGMA/Corbis,
(BL) ©Stocktrek/Corbis, (TR) ©MSFC/NASA; 202 ©DK Images; **Chapter 7:** 203
©Richard T. Nowitz/Corbis; 205 Colin Keates/©DK Images; 207 (TR) Stephen
Oliver/©DK Images, (BR) ©Richard T. Nowitz/Corbis; 208 (BL) ©DK Images, (BR)
©Scott W. Smith/Animals Animals/Earth Scenes, (TL) Tim Ridley/©DK Images; 209
(TC) ©DK Images, (CL) Colin Keates/Natural History Museum/©DK Images; 210
(TR) Natural History Museum/©DK Images, (BL) ©Dennis C. Murphy, (BR) Harry
Taylor/Courtesy of the Royal Museum of Scotland, Edinburgh/©DK Images, (TL)
Hemera Technologies; 211 Natural History Museum/©DK Images; 212 (TL, C, CR)
©DK Images; 213 (TR, CR) ©DK Images; 214 (BL, CR) ©DK Images, (TL) Natural
History Museum/©DK Images; 215 (TL) ©DK Images, (C) Giuliano Fornari/©DK
Images; 216 (TL) ©Francois Gohier/Photo Researchers, Inc.; 217 (Bkgd, TR)
©The Natural History Museum, London; 218 ©DK Images; 220 (Bkgd) ©Pat
O'Hara/Corbis, (TL, BR) ©James L. Amos/Corbis, (CL) ©George H. H. Huey/
Corbis, (BL) Colin Keates/Natural History Museum/©DK Images; 221 ©Lowell
Georgia/Corbis; 222 (T, CR) ©DK Images, (CL) ©Richard T. Nowitz/Corbis, (BR)
©Layne Kennedy/Corbis; 223 (T, CL) ©DK Images; 224 (BR) ©David Muench/
Corbis, (BR) ©Peter Larson/Courtesy of the Black Hills Institute of Geological
Research, Inc., Hill City, SD, (CR) ©Philip Gould/Corbis, (T) Senekenberg Nature
Museum/©DK Images; 226 Getty Images; 228 Colin Keates/Natural History
Museum/©DK Images; 230 Brand X Pictures; 231 Getty Images; 232 Digital
Vision.

Unit C: Divider: ©Matthias Kulka/Corbis; **Chapter 8:** 233 (C) ©Charles
Gupton/Corbis, (CR) Getty Images; 237 Getty Images; 239 (TR) Getty Images, (B)
Brand X Pictures; 242 Hemera Technologies; 244 ©DK Images; 248 Steve Gorton
and Gary Ombler/©DK Images; 250 Brand X Pictures; 252 ©Brand X Pictures/
Getty Images; 253 ©Craig Tuttle/Corbis; 254 ©Nedra Westwater/Robert Harding
Picture Library, Ltd.; 256 ©Royalty-Free/Corbis; 262 (B) ©ESA/PLI/Corbis, (TR,
R) ©DK Images, (BL) ©John F. Kennedy Space Center/NASA, (BR) ©The Boeing
Company; 263 (R) ©DK Images, (TR) Corbis, (C) NASA, (TL) NASA Image
Exchange; 264 (Bkgd) Getty Images, (B) ©JPL/Cornell/NASA, (CL) NASA, (BR)
©NASA/Corbis, (TL) Corbis, (B) ©ESA/PLI/Corbis; **Chapter 9:** 265 (C) ©Kelly-
Mooney Photography/Corbis, (TC) ©Stone/Getty Images, (T) ©Jim Cummins/
Corbis, (BR) ©Tom Stewart/Corbis, (BL) Getty Images; 267 (CR) ©Richard
Megna/Fundamental Photographs, (BR) ©Craig Tuttle/Corbis, (BL) Veer, Inc.; 269
©Jim Cummins/Corbis; 270 ©Jim Cummins/Corbis; 271 (BR) Getty Images, (TR)
Hemera Technologies; 272 (BL) ©Roger Ressmeyer/Skylab/NRL/NASA/Corbis,
(TL) Hemera Technologies, ©Tom Stewart/Corbis; 273 Getty Images; 274 Hemera
Technologies; 275 (TL) Corbis, (BL) ©John Conrad/Corbis, (TR) ©Laureen March/
Corbis, (BR) ©Jon Feingersh/Corbis; 276 Hemera Technologies; 278 (TL) Dave
King/Pitt Rivers Museum/University of Oxford, Oxford/©DK Images; 279 ©Tom
Stewart/Corbis; 280 Hemera Technologies; 281 ©Paul Seheult/Eye Ubiquitous/
Corbis; 282 (TL) Hemera Technologies, (B) ©Richard Megna/Fundamental
Photographs; 283 ©Royalty-Free/Corbis; 284 (TL) Hemera Technologies, (BL)
©Craig Tuttle/Corbis, (BR) ©Lonny Kalfus/Getty Images; 285 ©DK Images; 286
Getty Images; 287 (TL) ©Randy Lincks/Corbis, (TR) ©Tony Freeman/PhotoEdit,
Digital Vision; 288 (CL) Steven Gorton and Gary Ombler/©DK Images, (CL) Getty
Images; 289 Getty Images; 292 ©Bryn Colton/Assignments Photographers/
Corbis; 294 (CL) ©Richard Megna/Fundamental Photographs, (CC) Getty Images,
(BR) Veer, Inc.; 295 (TR) Hemera Technologies, (T) Getty Images; 296 (T, CR) Veer,
Inc., (CR) ©Robert Landau/Corbis, (Bkgd) ©Ken Davies/Masterfile Corporation,
(BL) ©Hans Neleman/Getty Images; **Chapter 10:** 297 (CC) ©Lester Lefkowitz/
Corbis, (TR) Getty Images; 298 (Bkgd) ©Paul Barton/Corbis, (T) Getty Images; 301

Getty Images; 302 (C) Getty Images, (Bkgd) ©Paul Barton/Corbis; 303 (TR) ©DK Images, (B) Getty Images; 304 (CL) ©Joyce Choo/Corbis, (R) ©First Light/Corbis, (TL) Getty Images; 306 (R) ©Chris Carroll/Corbis, (TL) Hemera Technologies, (BL) ©Stone/Getty Images; 307 (CR) ©DK Images, (CL, CR) Hemera Technologies; 308 (B) ©Wally McNamee/Corbis, (TL) Getty Images; 309 ©Stone/Getty Images; 310 Hemera Technologies; 311 ©Chapman/NewSport/Corbis; 312 Hemera Technologies; 313 (T) ©Mike Brinson/Getty Images, (B) ©ThinkStock/SuperStock; 314 Hemera Technologies; 316 (CL) ©Laurie Campbell/NHPA Limited, (CR) Getty Images; 317 (CL) ©Juergen & Christine Sohns/Animals Animals/Earth Scenes, (CR) ©Jonathan Blair/Corbis; 318 Gary Ombler/©DK Images; 320 Hemera Technologies; 322 Digital Vision; 326 (C) Getty Images, (TC) ©Joyce Choo/Corbis, (BR) ©Michael S. Yamashita/Corbis; 328 (C) Corbis, (TL) ©Jeff Caplan/Langley Research Center/NASA; **Chapter 11:** 329 ©John Gillmoure/Corbis; 330 (B) ©Martin Harvey/NHPA Limited, (T) ©Thinkstock; 331 ©Mark Boulton/Photo Researchers, Inc.; 333 (Bkgd) ©Thinkstock, (C) ©Tom & Dee Ann McCarthy/Corbis; 334 ©Thinkstock; 335 (TR) Getty Images, (B) ©Thinkstock; 336 (CL) ©DK Images, (CR) ©Jeff Hunter/Getty Images, (BL) ©Walter Hodges/Corbis, (TL) Getty Images, (BR) ©George Hall/Corbis; 337 (CL, BL) Getty Images, (CR, BR) ©Royalty-Free/Corbis; 338 (TL) Hemera Technologies, (B) ©DK Images; 339 (TR) ©Mark Boulton/Photo Researchers, Inc., (TL) Getty Images; 340 (CL) ©Roger Wilmshurts/Frank Lane Picture Agency/Corbis, (BL) Digital Vision, (TL) Getty Images; 341 ©Jeffrey L. Rotman/Corbis; 342 (TR) ©Royalty-Free/Corbis, (BL) ©Stephen Dalton/NHPA Limited, (CC) ©Image Quest 3-D/NHPA Limited, (CL) ©DK Images, (TL) ©Ingram/Creatas, (CL) Getty Images, (CL) ©Stockbyte; 343 (CR) ©Brownie Harris/Corbis, (TR) Corbis; 344 ©DK Images; 346 ©DK Images; 348 ©Tom Tracy/Corbis; 350 (BR) Digital Vision, (CL) ©DK Images, (CR) Getty Images; 351 (TL) ©DK Images, (C) Getty Images, (TR) ©Image Quest 3-D/NHPA Limited; 352 (Bkgd) ©Royalty-Free/Corbis, (B) ©Photex/S. Maka/Zefa/Masterfile Corporation, (CR) ©Alejandro Purgue; 353 PhotoLibrary; 354 (BCL) ©Paul Barton/Corbis, (BL) ©Thinkstock, (CL) ©Jim Cummins/Corbis, (CL) Getty Images; 355 ©DK Images; 356 ©Darwin Wiggett/Corbis; 358 (C, BL) Getty Images; 360 (Bkgd) ©Steve Satushek/Getty Images.

Unit D: Divider: (Bkgd) ©Reuters/Corbis, (BR) Corbis; **Chapter 12:** 361 (C) NASA Image Exchange, (TR) Getty Images; 362 ©Roger Ressmeyer/Corbis; 363 (BL) NASA Image Exchange, (BR) ©John Sanford/Photo Researchers, Inc.; 365 (Bkgd) ©Roger Tidman/Corbis, (TR) Getty Images; 366 ©Roger Tidman/Corbis; 367 ©SOHO (ESA & NASA)/NASA; 368 ©SOHO (ESA & NASA)/NASA; 372 (CL) ©John M. Roberts/Corbis, (BL) ©Royalty-Free/Corbis, (CR) Getty Images; 373 ©James Randklev/Visions of America/Corbis; 376 ©Roger Ressmeyer/Corbis; 377 ©Jerry Schad/Photo Researchers, Inc.; 378 NASA Image Exchange; 379 ©Stone/Getty Images; 380 ©John Sanford/Photo Researchers, Inc.; 381 ©Goddard Space Flight Center/NASA; 384 ©Roger Ressmeyer/Corbis; 386 ©Scott Tysick/Masterfile Corporation; 388 (BR) ©Roger Tidman/Corbis, (TR) ©Jerry Schad/Photo Researchers, Inc., (CL) ©John Sanford/Photo Researchers, Inc., (CC) NASA Image Exchange; 389 (CC) Getty Images, (CL) ©SOHO (ESA & NASA)/NASA, (TR) ©Goddard Space Flight Center/NASA; 390 (C) ©Denis Scott/Corbis, (T) Getty Images; 391 (T) ©GSFC/NASA Image Exchange, (B) ©Jet Propulsion Laboratory/NASA Image Exchange; 392 (CL) NASA, (BL) ©Bill Ross/Corbis, (Bkgd) ©Greatest Images of NASA/NASA Image Exchange, (TR) Getty Images; **Chapter 13:** 393 (C) ©Reuters/Corbis, (TL) ©Stone/Getty Images; 394 (BR) ©David Ducros/Photo

Researchers, Inc., (BL) ©Steve Raymer/Corbis, (T) ©Reuters/Corbis; 395 ©David Young-Wolff/PhotoEdit; 397 (TR) ©Stone/Getty Images, (CL) ©DK Images, (Bkgd) ©Reuters/Corbis; 398 ©Reuters/Corbis; 399 Hemera Technologies; 400 (TR) ©David Mace/Robert Harding Picture Library, Ltd., (BR) ©Giulio Andreini, (TL) Hemera Technologies; 401 (TL) Getty Images, (BL) ©Reuters/Corbis; 402 (CR) ©Steve Raymer/Corbis, (TL) Hemera Technologies, (B) ©Royalty-Free/Corbis, (B) Getty Images, ©Lester Lefkowitz/Corbis,©DK Images; 403 ©Bob Daemmrich/The Image Works, Inc.; 404 (BR) ©Science Museum/Science & Society Picture Library, (TL) Hemera Technologies, (BL) Getty Images; 405 (C) Getty Images, (TR) Unisys Corporation; 406 (B) ©DK Images, (TL) Getty Images; 407 (CR) ©David Ducros/Photo Researchers, Inc., (C) ©David Young-Wolff/PhotoEdit, (CL) ©Bob Daemmrich/Stock Boston; 408 (CL) ©DK Images, (TL) Getty Images; 409 ©DK Images; 410 ©Chuck Elliott/Getty Images; 412 ©Michael Newman/PhotoEdit; 413 (TC) ©Royalty-Free/Corbis, (CR) ©LWA-Dann Tardif/Corbis, (BL) ©Ariel Skelley/Corbis, (TL) ©Hutchings Stock Photography/Corbis; 414 (TC) ©Bob Daemmrich/Stock Boston, (TR) ©Reuters/Corbis, (C) ©Steve Raymer/Corbis, (CR) ©David Ducros/Photo Researchers, Inc., (B) Getty Images; 415 Brand X Pictures; 416 (B) ©Jet Propulsion Laboratory/NASA Image Exchange, (TL) NASA; 417 ©Arthur Tilley/Getty Images; 418 ©Roger Tidman/Corbis; 419 (TR) ©Stockbyte, (TR) Getty Images; 420 ©Benelux Press/Index Stock Imagery; 420 ©Royalty-Free/Corbis; 422 ©Stone/Getty Images; 423 (C) ©Stone/Getty Images, (C) Getty Images; 424 (R) ©Stone/Getty Images, (C) ©John W. Bova/Photo Researchers, Inc., (B) Getty Images.

End Matter: EM2 ©Tom Brakefield/Corbis; EM3 (BR) Jean-Louis Le Moigne/NHPA Limited, (TR) ©Don Enger/Animals Animals/Earth Scenes; EM4 (CR) ©Clem Haagner/Gallo Images/Corbis, (BR) ©DK Images, (TR) Veer, Inc., (BCR) NASA Image Exchange, (TCR) ©Roger Ressmeyer/Corbis; EM5 (BR) ©Grant Heilman/Grant Heilman Photography, (TR) ©Jim Cummins/Corbis, (CR) ©Reuters/Corbis; EM6 (T) ©The Image Bank/Getty Images, (BR) ©DK Images; EM7 (TR) ©Royalty-Free/Corbis, (TR) ©Joe McDonald/Corbis, (TR) ©Gaoil Shumway/Getty Images, (CR, B) ©DK Images, (BCR) ©Joyce Choo/Corbis; EM8 (TR) ©Mike Brinson/Getty Images, (BR)©DK Images, (TR) ©Tom Stewart/Corbis; EM9 (TR) ©Stone/Getty Images, (TCR) ©Marty Stoufer/Animals Animals/Earth Scenes, (BCR) Getty Images; EM10 (TR) ©DK Images, (CR) ©Soames Summerhays/Photo Researchers, Inc., (CR) ©DK Images, (BR) ©A & J Verkaik/Corbis; EM11 (BR) Joe McDonald/Corbis, (TR) ©DK Images; EM12 ©Bob Daemmrich/Stock Boston; EM13 (TR) Getty Images, (TCR) ©Owaki-Kulla/Corbis, (BR) ©Robert Thompson/NHPA Limited; EM14 (TCR) ©Richard T. Nowitz/Corbis, (BCR) ©John Sanford/Photo Researchers, Inc., (CR, BR) ©Mark Boulton/Photo Researchers, Inc.; EM15 (CR) William Bernard/Corbis, (BR) ©Stephen Frink/Corbis, (TR) ©Charles E. Rotker/Corbis, (BR) ©Randy Morse/Animals Animals/Earth Scenes; EM16 ©Pete Soloutos/Corbis, (CR) ©Richard Megna/Fundamental Photographs, (BR) Joe McDonald/Corbis; EM17 (TR) ©DK Images, (BCR) ©Owaki-Kulla/Corbis, (BR) ©David Ducros/Photo Researchers, Inc.; EM18 (TCR) ©Carol Cohen/Corbis, (CR) ©Craig Tuttle/Corbis, (BR) Getty Images; EM19 ©DK Images; EM20 (TR) ©Alan. R. Moller/Getty Images, (CR) ©Giulio Andreini, (BR) ©Steve Raymer/Corbis; EM21 (TR) ©Thinkstock, (TCR) ©Sam Abell/NGS Image Collection, (BCR) ©Owaki-Kulla/Corbis, (BR) ©Wally McNamee/Corbis

End Sheets: ES2 ©Tim Flach/Getty Images